AF528470

Encyclopaedia of Child Labour

Encyclopaedia of Child Labour

Volume-2

Case Studies and Legal Interventions

Promila Mahajan
S. Chand

Adhyayan Publishers & Distributors
Delhi-110094

Published by
ADHYAYAN PUBLISHERS & DISTRIBUTORS
L-9 B, Street No. 42, Sadatpur Extension
Delhi-110094
Ph.: 011-22191282, Fax : 011-22199182
E-mail : adhyayanpublishers@yahoo.com

Encyclopaedia of Child Labour
(2 Vols.)

Ist Edition : 2006
ISBN - 81-89161-77-6 (Set)

Printed in India

Published by Harish Chandra Yadav for Adhyayan Publishers & Distributors, Laser Typesetting at Himanshu Printers and Printed at Tarun Offset Printers, Delhi.

Preface

The future of any nation depends upon the sound development of children. As Wordsworth has also said 'Child is the Father of Man'. For construction of civilized, cultural and happy society, we have to educate and train our children properly because tomorrow they would take the nation towards prosperity. The ilimenation of child labour and their rehabilitation has emerged as an important area of scientific work. It has been seen that a large number of child labour are surviving under great health and safety hazards. Above all the workplace trauma is widespread, stunting the growth of the child both physically and mentally.

Hence, considering the problem in its totality, an effort has been made to cover the diverse aspects of the subject. All the articles are judiciously selected from authoritative sources. We are grateful to all the learned authors and academicians whose writings are cited or substantially made use of in these volumes. This Encyclopaedia has been divided into two volumes in which each volume is complete in it self.

They are as follows:

1. Status of Child Labour
2. Case Studies and Legal Interventions

This joint effort has been taken as an academic exercise to provide an over all view on issues and problems related to child labour at macro, meso and micro level, including the valuable contributions from social scientists, planners and administrators to present a more comprehensive view on the subject.

Students, teachers, researchers, administrators, policy planners and professionals from different streams of disciplines would find this Encyclopaedia informative and useful.

The Editors are also very grateful to Shri Harish Chandra Yadav of Adhyayan Publishers & Distributors, Delhi for taking keen interest in publishing it in very short time.

Promila Mahajan
S. Chand
Editors

Contents

1

Child Labour in Agriculture Sector

The child work force constitutes 6 per cen. of the total work force in the country and as many as 92 percent of child workers are engaged in agricultural and allied structures (Narayan,1980). About 8 per cent are employed in allied activities like hunting, fishing, livestock breeding, plantation labour, etc (Kulshreshtha, 1978), According to an International Labour Organization report (1979), as many as one-third of the rural children aged between 10 and 14 years and one-eight of urban children are at work in India. They contribute about 14 per cent of the income and largely belong to lower income groups of families (Gupta,1979). This indicates the significance of child labour force in the production and reproduction processes. The changes that have appeared since mid-1960s in the Indian agriculture, marked by enhanced commercial farming and green revolution, made the rural rich richer and poor poorer (Pattnaik, 1987) While this experience is, by and large, shared throughout Indian, the greatest inequality and class differentiation have occurred in the fastest growing areas. This however did not give the labourers the much talked about freedom from obligations under capitalism. Massive unemployment and underemployment, highly uneven capitalist growth, discovery of profitable uses of pre-capitalist relations of production, contributed to the growth of primitive accumulation of capital. Informal and unorganized labour market has grown phenomenally, so also the contrast and seasonally migrant labour. The employment of children too has increased and they are indeed preferred in certain agricultural and industrial operations.

One of the study carried out in Orissa by Sahoo (1995), in the two villages, there are 301 child workers, below the age of 15, distributed among 252 households. In other words, nearly half of the families have child workers. About 82 per cent of these families have a single child worker each. These include 12 girls of Chhadadiapalli who are actively engaged in agricultural operation along with their mothers. Forty families contain two child farm workers each and five families have three child labourers and none more than that.For the purpose of the study, four girls and 248 boys belonging to 252 families were selected. That means one each from a family containing child farm labour was chosen for detailed investigation. A few of them work in their own family only(1.9%), while others both in own fields as well as others' fields (71.8%) or only in others field(26.2%). Besides, children also perform a wide spectrum of domestic chores,though such labour is never measured in economic terms. In fact, even in the analysis of Agrarian structure the contribution of children and the possibilities of mobilizing their underutilized labour for economic development are generally overlooked.

Socio-Economic Background

Generally, the prevalence of child labour is attributed to the poverty of the individual households and backwardness of the regional society. Indeed, almost all studies on child labour in India have axiomatized that poverty coupled with illiteracy and unemployment compel the families to send their beloved children into the vortex of unjust labour market. There is after all a considerable body of factual and qualitative information to support. Nonetheless, the correlation, based on just two indicators and separated from the total socio-historical context conceal more than what it really reveals. This is more pertinent especially when poverty is a very relative term bound by a given time and space. As both poverty and illiteracy change with changes in socio-economic configurations, any scientific work demands analysis of social formations for the comprehension of the nature and extent of employment of children.

In Chhadiapalli and Kulanda, there are 164 and 137 child workers respectively. The 128 child workers from the former village and 124 from the latter were selected. In other words, 49.5 per cent of households in the two selected villages have at least one child worker each. Except the Brahmins, all castes and tribes have child workers. But there is a significant difference in the nature of employment of the children belonging to enterprising peasant castes and other castes and communities. Children of the former group mostly work in their own fields while the children of lower castes and tribes largely sell their labour to affluent farmers. About 83 per cent of the fathers of the child workers are illiterate and those few literate have not studied beyond primary school level. Indeed, only 2 per cent of them have studied up to standard V. That means the literate parents are,in fact, barely literate. Those belonging to peasant castes have relatively better representation in such level of literacy than the lower castes and tribes (Table 1). Nevertheless, the point is that the parents of child workers are conspicuously illiterate or barely literate.

Table 1:*Castes and Literacy of Parents of Child Workers*

Case	No. and percentage of families with child labour child workers	No. and percentage of literacy among the parents of
Brahmin (N=28)	Nil	Not Application
Kulata (N=97)	17 (17.5)	6 (35.3)
Belama (N=58)	20 (34.5)	12 (60.0)
Dumal (N=74)	28 (37.8)	8 (28.6)
Kalinji (N=39)	24 (61.5)	6 (25.0)
Alia (N=30)	25 (83.3)	4 (16.0)
Odiya (N=14)	10 (71.4)	Nil
Teli (N=10)	9 (90.0)	2 (22.0)
Telenga (N=16)	6 (37.5)	Nil
Gouda (N=17)	14 (82.3)	1 (7.1)
Gudia (N=6)	2 (33.3)	Nil
Bhandari (N=4)	2 (50.0)	Nil
Keuta (N=77)	10 (58.8)	Nil
Khadala (N=31)	27 (87.1)	2 (7.4)
Scheduled Castes (N=46)	40 (87.0)	2 (5.0)
Scheduled Tribes (N=22)	18 (81.8)	Nil
Total (N=509)	252 (49.5)	43 (17.1)

The occupational background of the families of child

workers reveals that only about 22 per cent belong to those families whose primary occupation is cultivation while secondary occupation is wage labour. They primarily belong to the traditional peasant castes. In contrast, 40 per cent of child workers belong to wage labour families. And about 38 per cent belong to families with wage labour as primary and cultivation secondary (Table 2). We have already noted that though all castes have child employment (except the Brahmin), none of the child workers of Kulata, Belama, Dumal, Kalinji and Telenga belong to wage labour families. In fact, primary occupation happens to be cultivation for most of the Kulata and Belama households whose children are engaged in labour in their own farms. The lower castes and tribes mostly belongs to agricultural labour and small peasant families. Hence, internal differentiation in the nature of child employment and its association with the caste hierarchy is very explicit.

Table 2:*Caste-Wise Occupational Distribution of Parents of Child Workers*

Cultivation Caste/Occupation	Wage primary and wage labour secondary	labour primary and cultivation	Wage labour only secondary
Brahmin (Nil)	-	-	-
Kulata (N=17)	14 (82.3)	3 (17.7)	-
Belama (N=20)	15 (75.0)	5 (25.0)	
Dumal (N=28)	13 (46.4)	15 (53.6)	-
Kalinji (N=24)	3 (12.5)	21 (87.5)	-
Alia (N=25)	4 (16.0)	13 (52.0)	8 (32.0)
Odiya (N=10)	-	3 (30.0)	7 (70.0)
Teli (N=9)	2 (22.2)	4 (44.4)	3 (33.3)

Telenga (N=6)	3 (50.0)	3 (50.0)	-
Gauda (N=14)	- (35.7)	5 (64.3)	9
Gudia (N=2)	-	2 (100.0)	-
Bhandari (N=2)	-	-	2 (100.0)
Keuta (N=10)	-	3 (30.0)	7 (70.0)
Khadala (N=27)	-	9 (33.3)	18 (66.7)
Scheduled Castes (N=40)	1 (2.5)	6 (15.0)	33 (82.5)
Scheduled Tribe (N=18)	-	3 (16.7)	15 (83.3)
Total (N=252)	55 (21.8)	95 (37.7)	102 (40.5)

$X^2 = 114.75$ df= 56 $p<.01$

Expectedly, most of the working children belong to families with no land or small uneconomic holdings. Forty per cent of the child workers hail from landless families and 45 per cent from households with less than one acre holding each, whereas only 4 per cent belong to households owning over 3 acre of land. Similarly, while none of the children of capitalist landlords and rich peasants are engaged in productive work, not even in their own farms, 55 per cent of child workers belong to farm worker and 41 per cent to small peasant families (Table 3).

Table 3: Class & Land Position of the Families of Child Workers

Class	No land	Upto1	1-2 acre	2acre+	Total
Capitalist landlord (N=11)	-	-	-	-	-
Rich peasant (N=41)	-	-	-	-	-
Middle peasant (N=92)	-	-	-	10	10 (4.0)
Poor peasant (N=142)	-	76	27	-	103 (40.9)

Farm workers (N=223)	102	37	-	-	139 (55.2)
Total (N=509)	102	113	27	10	252 (100.1)

$X^2=175.91$ df= 45 $p<.01$

If annual family income of Rs.5,000 is considered minimum need for an average sized family to cross the poverty line, then only about 5 per cent of the families of child workers belong to that category (Table 4). In fact, more than one-third of the families have an annual income of less than Rs.3,000. While 30 per cent of the families owning land above 3 acre each have more than Rs.5,000 annual income, the said percentage is less than 3 among the landless and very small peasants. In any case, their belonging to low income, poverty stricken groups is obvious.

Table 4: Annual Income of Families of Child Workers by Land Size (in Rupees)

Landsize	Upto 2000	2000-3000	3000-4000	4000-5000	Above 5000	Total
No land	15	27	48	9	3	102
Upto 1 acre	7	36	50	17	3	113
1-2 acre	-	5	6	11	5	27
2 acre+	-	-	1	6	3	10
Total	22 (8.7)	68 (27.0)	105 (41.7	43 (17.1)	14 (5.6)	252 (100.0)

$X^2=140.28$ df= 30 $p<.01$

Not only they belong to landless or small peasant and poor families who cannot reproduce themselves without introducing their children into the labour process but also as many as one-fifth of these families have sold their tiny parcels of land during the decade 1975-85. Of course, less than 4 per cent of the families have also added small fragments of dry land. A couple of families could indulge in this unusual practice of buying land because of remittances from the migrant workers of their families. Anyway, this is insignificant. About 22.2 per cent of the families have leased-in some land from the capitalist landlords and rich peasants as well as from some of the kin members who have migrated to distant places for employment. These sharecroppers mostly (77%) leased-in less than one acre of land. Those few leased-in more land belong largely to traditional peasant castes like Kulata and Belama. The higher castes and middle peasants normally employ their children in their own fields while the lower caste landless and small peasants tend to send their children for wage employment. The primary objective in the latter case is to supplement the family income. Tenancy does not provide a marked solution to the problem of wage employment of children.

With reference to the debt of the families of child workers, it is found that as many as 83.3 per cent are indebted. Moreover, 70.6 per cent of the indebted families have taken loans in both cash and kind from moneylenders, who are also the members of affluent agrarian classes-cum-speculative traders. The liberal institutional credit is insignificant in comparison to usurious moneylenders. It may be worth noting that 40 per cent of those who sold their lands during 1975-85 did so just to repay the earlier debt. The inter linkage of caste, land, credit and labour market ensures and reproduces a form of semi-feudal bondage. Here, the labour of children is often used as pawn to procure loans an even to lease-in land. In spite of the pompous declaration of the government to save the rural poor from the clutches of moneylenders, the small peasants and moneylenders to meet their immediate survival needs. Sometimes, to repay an earlier loan, a new is taken from some other moneylender. This debt trap reduces them to perpetual indebtedness. As a result, the bankrupt families are often forced to sell or mortgage their tiny landholdings or even family members.

Nonetheless, the amount of loan appears quite low that 58.7 per cent of the families have a loan of less than Rs.600. Only 4 per cent of the families, all belonging to Kulanda, have taken loans over Rs.1,000 (Table 5). But the point is that given their low family income and negligible immovable as-sets, the amount of loan is considerable. Moreover, the compound rate of interest fattens the original loan amount very rapidly. For instance, during the rainy months, just a couple of months before the harvest, the small peasants and tenants often take paddy loans under the condition that soon after the harvest they will return it in paddy calculated in terms of one and half times the original price. Not only 50 pre cent interest is charged for three to four months but also the calculation being made in terms of cash at pre-harvest and post-harvest times, actually doubles the repayment. Similar is the case with regard to agricultural inputs.

Table 5: Amount of Loan Taken by the Parents of Child Workers

Amount of loan (in Rs.)	Krlanda	Chhadiapalli	Total
Upto 200	10	11	21 (08.3)
200-400	22	37	59 (23.4)
400-600	30	38	68 (27.0)
600-800	12	18	30 (11.9)
800-1000	14	8	22 (08.7)
1000+	10	-	10 (04.0)
Not applicable	26	16	42 (16.7)
Total	124 (49.2)	128 (50.8)	252 (100.0)

The household consumption requirement is the major cause (25.8%) of loans, followed by marriage (16.7%), agricultural expenses (13.5%) and purchase of land and cattle (8.7%) (Table 6). As many as 45 per cent of indebted households have not repaid even a part of the loan and others have paid only a portion of the debt. In other words, most parents of child a workers, being always in debt, find no other alternative than seeking supportive hand from their children to augment survival of the families.

Given the fact of their poverty, illiteracy, low social and economic position, perpetual indebtedness, continued dependence on the rich to eke out a living, it is not surprising that over 96 per cent of the parents do not have membership in any formal institutions of the village.

Table 6:Purpose of Loan of the Parents of Child Workers

Purpose	Kulanda	Chhadiapalli	Total	No. Percentage	No. Percentage	No. Percentage
Husehold consumption	24	19.3	41	16.3	65	25.8
Marriage	14	11.3	28	21.9	42	16.7
Health	6	4.8	4	3.1	10	4.0
Agricultur expenses	19	15.3	15	5.9	34	13.5
Purchase of land or cattle	13	10.5	9	7.0	22	8.7
Education	8	6.4	6	4.7	14	5.5
Others	14	11.3	9	7.0	23	9.1
Not applicable	26	21.0	16	12.5	42	16.7
Total	124	49.2	128	50.8	252	100.0

Interestingly, when inquired why the children are sent to work, the parents one-fourth of the workers conveyed that it was to meet an obligation to their employers. Another 28 per cent pledged their children to repay their debts. Only 22 per cent disclosed poverty as the cause of child employment. About 12 per cent of the parents, mostly belonging to small-sized households, opined the necessity of assistance of their children in the farming operations and some 11 per cent justified it in terms of their children's poor performance at school (Table 7). In short, poverty and debt constituted the chief reasons for employment of children.

Further, when asked what are the major benefits they accrued from the employment of their children, over 40 per cent conveyed that they could procure loans easily. This is followed by financial help (32%), exchange of labour (14%) and supplementary help at work (13%). And when asked how the problem of employment of tiny children can be reduced, more than half of the parents opined that if only their economic condition improve (50.4%) and gainful employment at the rural set-up increases (23.0%). A quarter of the parents, however, told that rise of consciousness (13.5%), compulsory free and productive education (7.1%) and strict enforcement of the existing labour legislation (6.0%) may alleviate the problem.

Table 7:Reasons Given by Parents for Directing Children to Enter into Work force

Kulanda	Chhadiapalli	Total	Reasons	No. Percentage	No. Percentage	No. Percentage
obligation to employer	37	29.8	26	20.3	63	25.0
Repay the debts	34	27.4	37	28.9	71	28.2
Poverty	18	14.5	37	28.9	55	21.8
Need of assistance of children	28	18.5	7	5.5	30	11.9
Bad at school	8	6.4	19	14.8	27	10.7
Others	4	3.2	2	1.6	6	2.4
Total	124	100.0	128	100.0	252	100.0

However, without reiterating the obvious social and economic background of the child workers in the advanced agricultural set-ups let us analyze the nature of work and the terms and conditions of employment of children. Of course, the labour of children, both inside and outside the households, is always considered inferior to that of the adults. But the changes in production system and the socio-economic position of the child workers differentiate the degree and intensity of child labour. The nature and character of employment of children under subsistence economy, feudal system, and matured capitalist production system vary widely. Besides, the multi-structural formations provide a complex system of roles and statuses to different categories of child workers belonging to different strata of society.

Child Workers and their Work

The studied child workers belong to the age group between 8 and 15 years, but 72 per cent of them actually are within the range of 13 to 15 years, while 25 per cent are aged between 10 and 13 years, and 3 per cent come within the range of 8 to 10 years. Younger children sometimes attend school, besides helping in domestic chores and allied agricultural activities. Soon, however, they spend more time in productive and remunerative activities. It may not be out of place to recall the off repeated assertion that there is a negative correlation between child work and formal education, and extension of educational facilities constitutes one of the most effective remedies to the evil of child labour. This is simplistic and the correlation is superfluous. High drop-out and low attendance rates in the rural areas evidently suggest the importance of employment of children in the production process. Moreover, it is erroneous to presume that for the rural poor, education is an investment towards enhancing earning capacity. So long as education has a limited economic value, and contribution of children in the work process is considered essential, enhancement of educational facilities and forced enrollment will not be able to make any dent into the problem. Perhaps a reasonable suggestion could be restriction of hours of work for children, and restructurisation of school timings and curricula to impact essential ingredients of functional education in the shortest available time.

In all, 56 per cent of the child workers in the two village are illiterate. One-third have barely studied in the school. Only one-tenth of them have passed between standard III and V and none of them gone beyond the primary school level. The child workers of low caste families are mostly illiterate whereas those of the peasant castes are largely literate. For instance, illiteracy among child workers of Gudia and Bhandari households is cent-per cent. Those of the scheduled tribes are 89 per cent and scheduled castes 85 per cent, Khadala 81 per cent, Keuta 70 per cent, and so on. And the children who are literate have never gone beyond standard III. In contrast, all the child workers of Kulata caste are literate, 79 per cent in case of Kalinji, 75 per cent in case of Belama and 57 per cent of Dumal, are literate. Moreover, the child workers above standard III largely belong to these castes alone. The association between castes and educational status is significant. The fact that over 43 per cent of child workers are literate in an atmosphere of 70 per cent overall illiteracy may tempt some to presume that the child workers are relatively better placed in this regard. But this is incorrect. Free education and persuasion of the school teachers simply account for the marginal increase in literacy among the younger generation. The literate peasant caste child workers normally work in their own farms while illiterate or barely literate child workers belong to lower castes and tribes and mostly sell their labour power to others.

Notwithstanding the development of capitalism in agriculture, caste seems to continue to play a crucial role even with resect to the child labourers. As many as two-thirds of child workers engage in both their own farms and works as casual labourers of others peasants. They mainly belong to the peasant castes like Dumal, Kulata, etc, which are numerically as well as economically dominant in the village. They are now facing a pattern of immigration due to the technological growth in agriculture. In other words, they are both economically and socially better-off than the other castes' landless households. In contrast, most of the 30 per cent of child workers who rely on wage labour belong to the families of servicing castes, scheduled castes/tribes. They work largely as attached, semi-attached or contract labourers. Thus, there is a broad correlation between the caste status and degree of freedom of the child workers. This, however, does neither mean that the attached and semi-attached child workers are absent among the backward peasant castes nor does it convey that the lower caste child workers do not seek the greatest insecure contract and casual labour. It only highlights differential concentration of unpaid free child labour in terms of caste. Moreover, the fact that attached and semi-attached child workers are often employed in domestic chores and that purity and pollution still dictates social relationship in the village set-up, no matter whatever is the level of agricultural growth, there is also preference of workers of the same or upper caste than the lower caste. In case, however, the child workers are only needed to look after the cattle and carry out agricultural operations, preference is given to the lower caste whose employment is more advantageous to the employer than when one's own caste or of higher caste worker is employed.

Curiously, even the lower caste child worker prefer attachment to higher caste households than to the lower level, precisely because they cannot take water, let alone cooked food from the lower caste masters. In other words, besides the economic position, caste position dictates the child workers and their family members in the selection of the employer. If this relationship slightly weakened in the recent years, it is largely due to the growth of capital-intensive agriculture and changes in the need to employ any child worker for a longer time and mass immigration of outside labour. Also perhaps the land and labour legislations might have contributed to the apparent marginal alteration.

The child workers are internally differentiated in terms of their degree of attachment to the employers. This means not only the children and their involvement in the production is primarily decided by their parents in accordance with their socio-economic position but also their parents freedom to change the employers of their children is terribly restricted. Under such condition, of a scenario of multiple domination and dictation, the right of the children to choose their masters in terms of their own volition is immensely sabotaged. Table 8 indicates that 2 per cent of the child workers engage only in their own farms or tenanted lands. They belong to two traditional peasant castes. Attached and semi-attached child workers constitute half of the total underage workers. The remaining are casual wage earners. Attached labourer is defined here as the one who is employed by the employers on an annual basis or for an agricultural season. Their wage is fixed while the assignments remain unstructured, although a couple of primary works constitute the basis for decision on the quantum of wage. Among two-thirds of these cases, the attachments are usually renewed every year for a prolonged period. Only in exceptional cases, with the permission of the employer, they are allowed to sell their labour to others. In all but five cases, they are paid a fixed amount of cash and kind in several irregular installments during the contract period.

The amount depends on the age of the workers, status of the employers, major tasks assigned to him/her, and whether lunch is provided by the employer on the working days etc. Ironically the attached child workers and their parents, by and large, consider the attachment as a favour of the capitalist landlords and rich peasants. Besides, as nearly one-fourth of the attachments are related to current consumption loans and more than one-fifth to the conditions of whole debt, the notion of favour is reproduced. This may appear to convey that the relations of contract are based less on extra-economic coercions of the dominant class, than on mutual economic advantage to the employer and the employee. But the nature of the production system being such that the labour has little other means to secure livelihood than submitting to the demands of the ruling classes, who can go to any extent to preserve the unjust and obsolete order, cannot be ignored (Pathy, 1984).

Table 8: Caste and Pattern of Child Labour

Caste	Attached labour	Semi-attached labour	Casual labour	Labour in family farm
Brahmin (Nill)	-	-	-	-
Kulata (N=17)	11.8	29.4	58.8	-
Belama (N=20)	-	10.0	75.0	15.0
Dumal (N=28)	14.3	25.0	53.0	7.1
Kalinji (N=24)	8.3	12.5	79.2	-
Alia (N=25)	24.0	20.0	56.0	-
Odiya (N=10)	60.0	20.0	20.0	-
Teli (N=9)	33.3	44.4	22.2	-
Telenga (N=16)	-	66.7	33.3	-
Gauda (N=14)	21.4	21.4	57.1	-
Gudia (N=2)	-	100.00	-	-
Bhandari (N=2)	-	-	100.0	-
Keuta (N=10)	30.0	40.0	30.0	-
Khadala (N=27)	25.9	22.2	51.8	-
Scheduled Castes (N=40)	47.5	25.0	27.5	-
Scheduled Tribes (N=18)	61.1	22.2	16.7	-
Total (N=252)	26.2	24.2	47.6	2.0

$X^2 = 110.17$ df= 25 $p<.01$

The semi-attached child workers are operationally defined as those whose farm employment is based on monthly basis. In their case, the obligation to the master is relatively limited. Of course, a large number of them are not tied to their employers through credit nexus. Small peasants belonging to traditional peasant castes normally opt for casual wage labour along with their other family members. Evidently, attached and semi-attached child labourers mostly belong to the scheduled castes. Half of the child workers of Kulanda and more than one-third (37%) of Chhadiapalli are attached and semi-attached labourers. The wage rate for attached labourers is lower than the casual wage labourers, although the former perform more tasks and for longer periods of time. The rural credit system seen as the potent instrument to ensure the continued attachment,of the labourers. The loan demands not only exorbitant interests and multiple unpaid labour service but also the family measurement, manipulation of accounts an pricing system at different seasons, contribute to the perpetual indebtedness of the rural poor. In the village Kulanda, many of the tribal immigrant families do not possess house sites to their own. The landed interests of the village temporarily provide them sites for construction of house under condition that at least a member of their families be attached to them in return of food and festival gifts. This shows that capitalist landlords and rich peasants have found a cheap and profitable source of labour appropriation in the attached and semi-attached labour system.

Turning to the annual income of child workers (Table 9), Sahoo (1995), notice that as many as 30 per cent of them get less than Rs. 500. Indeed,36 per cent of attached and semi-attached workers belong to that income group while only 22 per cent of casual wage labourers have such meager income.. Nearly four-fifth of the child workers receive less than Rs. 700 each per annum. Only 5 per cent earn above Rs. 1,000 annually. Low wage is understandable, but in this case average per day income being around Rs. 1.60 indicates the extent of poverty, unemployment and destitution. On the days of farm employment, the child labour receives between Rs. 2 and Rs. 3 on an average as against Rs. 8 to Rs. 10 for male adult workers performing the same type of work. The wages are fixed arbitrarily and unilaterally. Along with such a less than subsistence wage, the frequent ill-treatment, the deplorable working condition and hours of work have endangered the physical, and mental health of the child workers. In any case, parents take away the wages of their children, except some pocket expenditure, during festival and other times.

Table 9: Nature of Child Employment and Annual Income

Nature of employment	Upto Rs. 500	500-700	700-900	900+	N.A.	Total
Attached labour	19	28	13	6	-	66
Semi-attached labour	27	25	9	-	-	61
Casual wage labour	27	70	15	8	-	120
Labour in own farm			-	-	5	5
Total	73 (30.0)	123 (48.8)	37 (14.7)	14 (5.6)	5 (2.0)	252 (100)

Immigration into the developed village of Kulanda by the poverty-stricken tribal and Harijans from the drought-prone neighboring areas has increased not only the employment of children but ironically more as attached and semi-attached labourers (50%). The other village with marked commercial agriculture has witnessed out migration of a substantial proportion of male adult work force to far distant semiskilled occupations and thereby raised the necessity of employment of more children but largely as free wage labourers (55%). The phenomenon of migration can no longer be explained simply in terms of' push' or' pull' factors (Todaro, 1976; Connell et al. 1976; Barik 1988). At this moment, it is probably difficult to say how the simultaneous migration and immigration shapes the division of labour between the children and adults and the forms of dominance in the village production system.

Nonetheless, the point is that the advancement of agriculture instead of declining the employment of tiny workers has in fact made them more vulnerable to economic and social exploitation. The major source of surplus appropriation still continues to be the cheap an unorganized labour force, in which children and women are most vulnerable. The labour saving modern mechanisms and inputs have not displaced the significance of cheap labour to the controllers of the productive assets. Besides, the survival of the small parcels of land demonstrates the need to utilize the domestic labour would further diminish the meager value of the produce. This indicates that articulation of capitalism has benefited from the use of backward forms and relations of production. There is thus no imminent need for the powers that be to transform or eliminate such atrocious institutions and relations.

Regarding the labour days spent in agriculture, it is found that one-third of the child workers get employment for over 200 days per year. This appears on the higher side of average employment available to agricultural workers in Indian rural context, irrespective of the level of development. But 80 per cent of all those who get such higher employment, actually are attached labourers who perform not only agricultural work but also domestic chores. Hence, greater employment at lower wage cost. Another one-third of child labourers get employment for 150 to 200 days per year, followed by 23 per cent between 100 to 150 to days, and about 9 per cent between 50 and 100 days(Table 10). Those who work between 150 and 200 days mostly belong to the families of less than 2 acre of landholding, and engage about 100 days in their own farms and rest in other fields. The primary employers for over half of the child workers (54%) belong to the class of rich peasants and 33 per cent by capitalist landlords, while 13 per cent by middle peasants. This shows the inclination of use cheap labour power for surplus product.

Beside farm work, they also indulge in stone cutting, brick making, canal digging, road construction and other non-agricultural summer activities. In fact, one-third of them work up to 30 days in non-agricultural occupations and one-fourth between 30 and 60 days (Table 11).

Table 10: Labour Days Spent in Agricultural Sector

Type of labour	Upto 100 days	100-150	150-200	200+	N.A.	Total
Attached	-	-	-	66	-	66
Semi-attached	5	32	24	-	-	61
Casual	17	26	60	17	-	120
Others (not available)	-	-	-	-	5	5
Total	22	58	84	83	5	252

These activities are contract works performed along with the family members and close kin groups. Here, they get a slightly better wage of about Rs. 4 per day but calculated in terms of piece rate. These works are also more strenuous than farm work. Besides the aforesaid works, child workers of small peasants and farm workers involve in caring livestock, collecting firewood, looking after the siblings, gathering fodder for cattle and so on. Although some of these activities are not strictly productive in the sense of generating income but are essential tasks for the reproduction of the households. Indirectly they are also production as by their engagement, they free other members of the households to engage in productive labour (White, 1975; Cain, 1977). Be that alone; the difference in the amount and type of work performed by children of land owning and landless families is, however, striking.

Table 11: Labour Days Spent in Non-Agricultural Wage Work

No. of days	Stone cutting	Brick making	Canal digging	Others	Not applicable	Total
Up to 30	5	22	19	35	-	81
30-60	8	22	16	25	-	71

60+	3	9	4	18	-	34
N.A.	-	-	-	-	66	66
Total	16	53	39	78	66	252

In the farm sector children engage in diversified activities. Considering the average child labour's involvement, it is found that he indulges in ploughing for 20 days, sowing eight days, harvesting 30 days and others like watching crops, weeding, measuring, leveling etc., around 50 days. Nearly 8 per cent of child workers said that last year they could not earn more because of frequent ill health. Time duration of payment of wages varies depending upon the contract between the employers and labourers. Only one-third of child workers are paid daily while the rest received after a long duration, including quarterly or half yearly. The mode of payment also varied primarily according to the nature of employment. They are paid in cash (15.1%) or kind (9.1%) or both (48.8%) or even in terms of repayment of loan (22.2%) and exchange of labour (4.8%).

Incidentally, 70 per cent of attached child labourers and half of the semi-attached labourers have also changed their employers; about 30 per cent once, 22 per cent twice, and 9 per cent thrice. This indicates that they are not employed recently, and that their dependence on a given employer is impermanent. Indeed, half of them changed due to low wages or violation of the oral contract and a quarter on account of excessive work and unreasonable behavior including physical assault, by the employers.

Weak economic background and credit nexus have forced them into the unjust labour market. Lack of consciousness and organizational activities and obviously the apathy of the state has aggravated the problem. Surprisingly, one-fifth of the child workers opined that they are not in a position to extrapolate their future and an equal number was not sure of finding any better alternative. They, of course, feel and desire for a respite from such hard and unremunerative work. The parents and relatives who ask the children to work are equally helpless themselves, and thus tend to console in terms of having an extra supportive hand to family income. Without repeating, it may be sufficient to note that the dominant assumption of agricultural growth declining the employment of under-aged workers and pre-capitalist relations of production is found untrue, in this study. Instead what is noticed is the co-existence of commercial agriculture with large-scale employment of children in both agriculture and non-agricultural sectors, and that too often under procapitalist obligations and relations. The pitiable working and living environment of the child workers can be made more explicit through a few case studies.

Case Studies

It may be useful to categorize the cases to arrive at a better comprehension of the phenomenon. Of course, as well be seen, the diverse cases essentially convey the overall trend in advanced agricultural context, which reproduces the employment of underaged work force at a cheaper rate and with multiple obligations. The first one comprises fifteen cases belonging to farm worker or poor peasant classes. They work mostly as attached or semi-attached to the capitalist landlords and rich peasants, and receive a relatively lower wage. Besides the tradition, the impoverishment of peasantry, artisan and servicing castes has facilitated their forced employment. The second category comprises two cases belonging to small and middle peasants' households, who face constant threat of unemployment, and work both on their own farms and hire out to other employers. The last category includes three cases where the children are compelled to accept familial responsibility due to some unexpected calamities at home and primarily engaged in self-cultivation.

Case-1

Ramesh Dakua (15) is a attached labourer to a Brahmin rich peasant of Chhadiapalli village. He belongs to Bhandari caste. His father and elder brother are working in some power loom units at Surat. He lives along with his mother and sister. Till recently his family had an acre of land and also leased in some land. The income from farming as well as rural wage being inadequate for the survival of the family, his parents incurred debts. Besides for the marriage of his brother the tiny farm was sold to a rich peasant. The two male adults migrated to Surat and Ramesh became attached to the Brahmin rich peasant. He says: "Because of the honesty and integrity of my father the Sahukar (the creditor / master) has given me the job and rejected the offers of other parents." Presumably, he considers getting the assignment as a credit. Anyway, he is primarily assigned the duty of herding the cattle and cleaning the cattle shed, but more often than not given unspecified agricultural and households chores from 7 a.m. to 7 p.m., without any fixed hours of break. Mother receives the wage, paid monthly or at times in shorter intervals upon request. During the Dasahara festival in October, the master giver him a pair of new clothes and a few extra coins. His mother often works as a casual worker in the farms of the rich peasant, though she receives a lower wage than the prevailing market rate. The immigration of his father and brother to Surat has not changed their condition of existence, and a major portion of the debt to the Brahmin rich peasant persist. He is told that the recurring illness of his father and frequent retrenchment of his brother forbade them to remit any appreciable amount of money to lessen their sufferings at home. Ramesh is unhappy due to the low wage and wishes to immigrate to some city but only if his father and brother permit.

Case-2

Subhash Das (13) is an illiterate attached labourer of Kalinji caste of Chhadiaplli. His father was a coal miner at Samastipur. At the age of eight, Subhash got his first employment as an attendant in the house of an officer of the mine. His salary was Rs. 50 p.m., besides food and other facilities. But as his father suffered from T.B., the family returned back to the native place. Meanwhile, an acre of land was purchased from the savings. Farming the land led the family to a debt trap and thus it is mortgaged. In order to pay the loan, Subhash is employed in the house of a capitalist landlord-cum-money lender. During the last two years several times he conveyed his unwillingness to work there but his father being promise bound has persuaded him every time. But now his father is arranging for his migration to Surat to work in a textile processing unit at Surat. He is looking forward for the freedom and better wage in Surat.

Case-3

Sudhakar Patra (16) is a semi-attached labourer in the house of a rich peasant of Mngalpur village. His family consisting of seven members own 1.25 acre of land. His father works at Surat an frequently remits money for household expense. In fact, Sudhakar having faired poorly in the school went to Surat to work along with his father. But within a year due to harsh working environment, twelve hour shifts and filthy living conditions without civic amenities, made him ill and thus returned to the village. At the moment he appears content working in his own field as well as in the rich peasants' frame. He says though the wages are low in the village, from the health point of view, it is far better than the city employment.Sudhakar's only concern in on the present and tomorrow is left to the consideration of the parents, particularly father.

Case-4

Ram Kunda (15) is an Semi-attached labourer to a capitalist landlord of Kulanda. Some two decades back his parents immigrated from Bolangir and worked as an agricultural labour in Baragarh region, followed by digging canal under a contractor. Since the age of none, Ram used to help his father, and subsequently he became an attendant in the common mess of the labour contractors. Working hours stretched from 6 a.m. to 8 p.m. with unspecified leisure time, depending on the availability of work. His monthly salary was Rs. 20 plus three times food. Lured bv the rich peasant of Kulanda, his father shifted to the village. Initially they received Rs. 500 as advance to be repaid through labour. Presently, his whole family comprising of parents, two sisters, three brothers and himself work in the land of rich peasant, and on an average receive around Rs. 20 per day. Ram is paid only Rs. 45 per month without food while his younger brother (10 years) is only given a meal per day. Ram washes clothes, cleans vessels, mopes house floor and does many unspecified works. He feels suffocated and cannot escape. Once in two or three years, the family visits their kites and kin in their ancestral village. The whole family is illiterate and none knows any civil and political rights.

Case-5

Bipin Das (15) is a literate (standard II level) attached labourer to a rich peasant of Kulanda. His joint family consists of seventeen members. Their small holding at Rangali of Sambalpur area forced the members to opt for diverse occupations. Bipin started as a railway employee's house at Jharsuguda with a monthly wage of Rs. 15 and food. After an year he shifted to a hotel of the same town with Rs. 50 salary and food. Ill-treatment and overwork forced him to join as a helper to a forest contractor-cum-capitalist landlord. His father was persuaded to be attached to his farm and accordingly five members of his family have shifted to Kulanda. All of them work for the capitalist landlord at a lower wage rate than the prevailing market rate. The household chores are unpaid except for occasional left over foods. Very often, the lady of the house scolds them. During the off season, they are allowed to work outside, and then Bipin earns an average of Rs. 6 to Rs. 7 on repairing canal and dam.

Case-6

Bipin Pradhan (17) is an illiterate tribal boy. His landless family having faced the constant atrocities of the forest contractor in the remote village of Sundargarh migrated to a construction site near the Rourkela Steel Plant, working under a contractor, Bipin used to receive Rs. 4 per day. Irregular payment and frequent denial of work, made them to leave the place. Along with his parents, he arrived Kulanda some three years back. Since then the whole family has been working for a given capitalist landlord. Bipin does not know specified life is no better than before, except for the availability of secured employment.

Case-7

Achutya Nag (13) belong to a five membered artisan family. Through his father suffers from a chronic stomach ailment, he continues to catty out the caste occupation both within and outside Chhadiapalli. His mother also suffers from chest pains. Due to their illness, the family incurred a debt and subsequently sold half and mortgaged the other half of the total one are holding. Elder brother also works in the family work occupation as well as goes to casual farm work. A chutya never entered school. He mostly goes for farm labour and receives between Rs. 3 and Rs. 4 a day. When hired to harvest sugar cane, he is paid Rs. 3 for every 100 bundles, each containing between 8 and 12 pieces of sugar cane. His wage then comes to about Rs. 6 Besides for carrying the bundles to the roadside he gets an extra wage of Re. 1 or Rs. 2, depending on the distance. The children are given this task only if they can carry at least 100 bundles a day. A chutya also helps mother in household work and wishes to practice his caste occupation.

Case-8

Dharanj Sahoo (14) is an illiterate attached labourer to a capitalist landlord. The contract is renewed annually and the wage adjusted as repayment of an outstanding loan. Curiously, neither Dharani knows the amount of debt nor how much is repaid. He only gets two meals in return for his back-breaking farm and non-farm jobs like tending animals, sweeping house, drawing water from the well, watering the vegetable garden on alternate days etc. He is nurturing a hope to migrate to Surat and escape from the drudgery.

Case-9

Muneshwar Das (14), a milkman by caste, belongs to a family of landless. For long the family was surviving on tending the cattle of the village and selling the milk from the four cows and three buffaloes, besides of course farm labour. As better milch cattle are bought by the affluent through bank loans, their survival support declined. Moreover, to meet the funeral expenses of grandmother, two cows were sold and a buffalo died of some unknown disease. Due to the fall of grazing land, fodder became costly. Muneshwar is looking after the cattle from early childhood but now he works as a casual labourer and gets employment for about 150 days per annum. During summer months he tends the cattle often better off peasants and gets Rs. 30 per month. He thinks of having one hybrid cow which would give ten liters of milk. But how can he and his family afford?

Case-10

Kameswar Rao (14) has studied upto standard V. He belongs to a Telugu migrant family. His father has purchased one and half acre of irrigated land and also leased-in another half an acre. Kameswar remains busy throughout the year in multi crop farming of their field. Sometimes he also participates in reciprocal labour exchange with some Telugu speaking small peasants. Roughly he spends 40 days per annum in others' fields on exchange basis and an equivalent number of days in Telugu rich peasant's farm to get a share in water and some modern inputs. Such non-waged labour relationship is, however, restricted only a few migrant families.

Case-11

Ravikanta (14) belongs to a small peasant family. His father worked also as a contract labourer in eastern Orissa and as a worker in Bihar coal mines. He used to remit money for family maintenance, and also managed to buy one and half acre of land. But, unfortunately, his father died in an accident in the mine. This forced Ravikanta, the eldest child to look after the family consisting of two brothers and two and two sisters. The farm is not adequate for the survival of the family and hence he also works as a labourer in others' fields. And yet, he has already borrowed heavily from the village moneylender. The marriage of the elder sister forced him to sell one-fourth acre of land to a rich peasant. Anyway, Ravikanta is pulling on disinterestingly without knowing the future.

Case-12

Brahmar Jena (15) a self-employed agricultural worker belongs to a small peasant-cum-tenant family. His father had worked in Assam and Asansol, but ill health forced him to return back to village. And then he went to Surat along with Brahmar, who became a twister in a small power loom unit. Both of them earned about Rs. 1,500 per month. Facing continues health problems, once again, they returned to native village. Brhmar works in his family farm, leased in farms and occasionally in others' fields. He says that the only thing they get from year long labour is just minimum food and clothing needs.

The case studies provide the implicit support to the quantitative information. Suffice here to note that rapid agricultural growth in the recent years has endangered the survival rights, of the children of exploited social class and status groups, and that their future, if any, is rendered bleak.

Conclusion

The observations will not only be as concise as possible, but also deliberately provocative, in the hope that it might encourage others to study these problems more closely. Nothing has been concluded of course. The discourse and dialogue do not end.

Despite the recent proliferation of child labour studies in India, there is a paucity of new ideas and insights into the process of the historical and social conditioning of the phenomenon. The conventional wisdom explains the existence and change of the phenomenon in terms of poverty, illiteracy, chronic unemployment,rapid demographic expansion,regional backwardness and apathy of the state. These factors,though crucial, are not sufficient for the comprehension of the nature and dynamics of employment of children. The treatment of the phenomenon in isolation from the larger historically evolved political economy provides little sociological insights into the issue. In other words, the conventional approach indicates only certain dimensions of phenomenal existence and conveys little about the structure of its reproduction. It is time to move beyond simple truisms to a more profound analysis of the mechanisms perpetuating the phenomenon of child labour. Not only the child labour studies refrain from holistic and historical analysis of the phenomenon but are also confined to urban unorganized sector which employs barely one-tenth of the total child work force. Meanwhile, agriculture and allied sectors which employs over 90 per cent of the under-aged work force has received little academic or political concern. In fact,there is almost little substantive research on child labour in advanced agricultural regions. Surprisingly, it has been found impossible to arrive at any generalized propositions on the formation, nature and character of child labour force; their structural position in the total production context, their consciousness, struggle and future. This study starved to formulate and develop new dimensions and approaches in the child labour research. It also questioned the widely held fallacious notion that agricultural growth would contribute to the decline of employment of children in productive process.Instead,this study has demonstrated that the nature of agrarian capitalism being primitive is prone to employ and expropriate the cheap labour,including that of the children.

The criterion of age has been euphemistically used as the sole indicator of determining the child on employment. This juridico-administrative demarcation is hardly sociologically convincing, for it ignores the socio-economic conditions circumscribed by culture, ideology and above all the production relations. The need to work-out an alternative to the prevailing age criterion and the over popularized notion of universal significance is strongly indicated.

This study has argued that the nature of child labour varies in space and time depending on the character and strength of the given political economy. The two major propositions—that higher the development of agriculture (primitive accumulation of capital), the greater is the peasant pauperization and consequent increased employment of children; and that uneven development of agriculture tends to larger recruitment of children into the underpaid force from among the lower classes and castes—are amply substantiated.

Nonetheless, there are quite a few important methodological problems in the study of class structure at micro level. This is precisely because of the openness of village agriculture in terms of labour and produce. Similarly, though noting the objective classes is inadequate to understand a class society, and that a complete picture demands the exploration of the mediation structure between objective classes and their consciousness and actions, it was rather found insurmountable to extrapolate the potentiality and trend of the structure. The apparent permanence of the system at the given moment is only partially responsible to this limitation. Besides village studies, howsoever powerful may be, can hardly extend in full strength to the regional political economy.

The multi-structural regional system has certainly not been able to disintegrate all forms and relations of pre-capitalism, rather has tended to co-exist with many of them albeit in slightly modified forms. This did not give the labourers the much talked about freedom from obligations. Meanwhile, severe unemployment and underemployment, uneven capitalist growth, discovery of profitable usages of pre-capitalist relations of production, and unorganized labour market contributed to the growth of primitive accumulation of capital,without the necessary strength to transform the absolute relations in the production.

The assumption that with the modernization of agriculture, the children will be rarely employed in the production, is found untenable. The children of capitalist landlords, rich peasants and Brahmins do not engage in farm work. Nearly 85 per cent of the child workers belong to farm worker and small peasant families of lower castes and tribes. Those who belong to peasant castes normally work in their own farms, though occasionally also hire out themselves. Mostly their parents are illiterate and poverty-stricken. During the last decade,one-fifth of these families have sold their tiny parcels of land. Moreover, 83 per cent are indebted, moslty to moneylenders and no wonder 28 per cent are employed to repay the debts. In fact, 40 per cent of the families of child workers said that the major benefit from the employment is to procure loan. Obviously, poverty,illiteracy,low social and economic position,perpetual indebtedness,etc.,forced them to employ their children to eke out a living. This conveys volumes on the nature and impact of agrarian capitalism.

Over one-fourth quarter of the children are of less than 13 years of age. None of the child workers have studied beyond primary school level while 56 per cent, largely belonging to lower castes and wage earning families,have never entered school. It is false to assume that extension of educational facilities would be one of the most effective deterrents to the evil of child employment. For the rural poor education is not an investment.

So long as education has a limited economic value and considered essential, educational expansion per cannot alter the situation.

There seems to be a broad correlation between the caste status and the degree of freedom of child workers. Of course,purity and pollution dictates employment of children for domestic labour but when they are needed for animal husbandry and farming, preference is given to lower castes. Surprisingly, half of the child workers are attached or semi attached whereas just 2 per cent work in their own farms. About half of the attachment is due to debt and consumption loan. Though their wages are low, curiously attachment to an employer is considered as a favour. Immigrant families from drought prone areas have been compelled to attach their children to capitalist landlords or rich peasants. About 80 per cent of child workers earn less than Rs.700 per annum. The average wage being Rs.1.60 indicates the extent of destitution. A casual child labour normally gets between Rs.2 and Rs.3 a day as against Rs.8 to Rs.10 for a male adult worker, performing the same type of work. One-third of them work over 200 days a year. The primary employers of child workers are the rich peasants (54 %), capitalist landlords (33 %) and middle peasants (13 %). Besides farm work and looking after cattle, many of them go for stone cutting, brick making, canal digging, road construction, etc., during summer months. There, of course, they work under labour contractor and along with their parents.

In short, advancement of agriculture,instead of declining the employment of tiny workers, has in fact made them more vulnerable to economic and social exploitation. While articulation of capitalism profitably used the cheap child labour of exploited social classes and status groups, the continuance of small holdings too necessitated the utilization of children in the farming. The future of these under-aged work force, if any, has been rendered bleak. Intervention of democratic institutions and processes may perhaps ease the situation, but as yet there is nothing in sight. But is appears that neither the employers nor the state on their own can take any decisive step towards solution of the problem without united challenges from the working people at large, supported by other democratic and progressive forces. Subjective benevolent intentions and endeavors can hardly resolve the issue.

2

Child Labour at Tea-Stalls Sweet-Shops & Dhabas

The institution of child labour in tea-stalls, sweet-shops and dhabas is not of recent origin. Its evidence has been found even in the earlier days of human civilization. The practice of engaging the labour of the children by the owners of the tea-stalls, sweet-shops and dhabas is the direct result of poverty and has thus become a chief source of the earning of the poorest elements of the society.

The mass exodus from Indian village is a well known phenomenon. It is now a widely accepted proposition that influx of people migrating to the cities is increasing on an unprecedented scale day-by-day. The cross over to the opportunities in the village on the one hand and tremendous pressure on land on account of population exploitation of the other. Reduced to the state of penury, these poor creatures are left with no other choice than to be migrated to the cities in search of living. It is well established fact that majority of the people of the village being ignorant, poor, illiterate, and having no exposure to the formal education can only lay their hands upon mental jobs as are performed by the child workers in the tea-stalls, sweet-shops and dhabas, etc. This probably explains to the large number of people taking to this profession as a means of their livelihood. It is equally true with their children also. At present, it is well proved fact that the child workers in the tea-stalls, sweet-shops and dhabas are not protected by any legislation. The result is that they are most exploited lot. In these establishments where the system of employing child labour is well established, the conditions of work and wages of these workers have not undergone any appreciable change over decades. Moreover, in the absence of any formal agreement between the child servant and his employer the term of employment are most arbitrary and exploitative and no job security is provided to them. They can be hired and fired on any flimsy pretext by their mighty employers. They have drudge right from early hours in the morning to late hours in the evening, with or without intermittent rest pauses, for pitifully low wages. They have often to work right through the months and through the years. The child labour legislations appear to have made a little dent on their life and the employers of these establishments enjoy a long rope in regulating their conditions work and wages.

It is difficult to make an authentic estimate of number of such servants in the country because the mass exodus to the cities is alarming. Child workers are like migratory birds who oftenly travel with the season. The Employment Exchanges (Compulsory Notification of Vacancies) Act, 1959 does not require notification of vacancies in these establishments. Nor is there such an obligation on the part of their employers to register the names of their servants with the appropriate authorities. For the reasons mentioned above, it is thus difficult to put forth an estimated number of such child workers.

FINDINGS OF THE SURVEY

The survey of 55 establishments revealed that 212 workers were working in these establishments, carrying out all sorts of jobs which include cooking, cleaning, sweeping, serving, preparation of the tea and sweets, etc. It is revealed from the survey that 80 child workers were engaged in various services by the owners of the tea-stalls, sweet-shops and dhabas. It is evident from the Table 1.

Table 1

Sr. No.	Nature of Establish-ments	Number of Establish-ments	Total	Adults Emplo-yees	Chil-dren	%
1	2	3	4	5	6	7
1.	Tea-Stalls	12	34	19	15	44.11
2.	Sweet-Shops	16	67	44	23	34.32
3.	Dhabas	27	111	69	42	37.87
	Total	55	212	132	80	

The study of Table 1 show that out of 212 total workers, the number of children was 80. It constitutes 37.73 per cent of the total employment given to the workers in the 55 establishments. The number of adult was 132 which comes to 62.27 per cent when compared with the child workers in the establishments surveyed.

Further, the study of Table 2 reveals that the mode of employment followed by the owners of the establishments are of three kinds, viz., (i) employment through self, (ii) employment through relationship, (iii) other sources. Out of 80 child workers, 20 have stated to have got employment through self-persuasions, 36 through their relationship, and remaining 24 were induced by the owners through other sources.

Table 2 : Mode of Employment

Sr. No.	Mode of Employment	No. of children	Percentage
1.	Self	20	25
2.	Through Relations	36	45
3.	Other Sources	24	30

Similarly, the study of Table 3 (given below) discloses that the wage-range of child workers varies from 0-350 rupees and above. Out of 80 child workers, 15 get their wages below 150 rupees, 44 child workers are given wages between rupees 150-250, 19 get their wages between rupees 250-350. There are only two child workers who have stated their wages above rupees 350. Thus, it is quite evident that only 2.5 per cent of working children get their salaries above rupees 350 and remaining 97.5 per cent child workers draw their wages below rupees 350. There are 23.75 per cent child-workers who have their wage between rupees 250-350 and 18.75 per cent get a poor wage of rupees 0-150 from their employers.

Table 3 : Detail of Wages earned by Children

Sr. No.	Wage Range in Rs.	No. of Children	Percentage
1	2	3	4
1.	Upto 150	15	18.75
2.	150-250	44	55.00
3.	250-350	19	23.75
4.	Above 350	2	2.50

It is also very much clear from the survey that the child workers of these establishments belong to different castes. Table 4 reveals that 68.75 per cent of the child workers are

Rajput, 20 per cent Brahmin, 10 per cent scheduled caste and schedule tribe and 1.25 per cent Muslims. Thus the study of Table 4 shows that 55 child labour belongs to Rajput families, 16 from the Brahamin, 8 from the scheduled caste and scheduled tribes and one from the Muslim.

Table 4: Caste of Child Workers

Sr. No.	Caste of Children	No. of Children	Percentage
1	2	3	4
1.	Rajput	55	68.75
2.	Brahmin	16	20.00
3.	Scheduled Castes Scheduled Tribes	8	10.00
4.	Muslim	1	1.25

Table 5 throws light on the age composition of the child workers in the 55 establishments surveyed by the researcher. During the survey it was found that 14 children were of 9 years of less than 9 years. It constitutes 17.5 per cent of the total child-workers interviewed, 38 children were between the age group of 9-12 years, it is 47.5 per cent, and 28 children were between the age group of 12-14 years which comes to 35 per cent of the total child workers in these establishments.

Table 5 : Age Composition of Child Workers

Sr. No.	Age range in years	No. of Children	Percentage
1	2	3	4
1.	Upto 9 years	14	17.5
2.	9-12	38	47.5
3.	12-14	28	35.0

The study of Table 6 shows the educational profile of child workers, in these establishments. It shows that 36 child workers, that is 45 per cent of the total child workers, were t otally elite, 35 child workers are those who had joined the study but could not complete even fifth standard. The percentage of these child workers is 43.75 per cent. It is also found that 9 child-workers are those who have though passed primary education but could not go beyond the middle standard. The percentage of these children is recorded as 11.25 per cent when compared with the total strength of the child workers of 55 establishments. However, none of the 80 child workers was matriculate or above. It is crystal clear from the educational profile of children given in Table 6.

Table 6 : Education Profile of Child Workers

Sr. No.	Education of Children	No. of Children	Percentage
1	2	3	4
1.	Not educated	36	45
2.	0-5th	35	43.75
3.	5th to 8th	9	11.25
4.	Above 8th	0	0

The study of Table 7 shows that out of 80 child workers 34 hail from Nepal, 10 from Bihar, 11 each from Shimla and Solan district, 4 each from Mandi and Sirmaur, 2 each from Hamirpur and Kangra, one each from Kullu and Una districts of Himanchal Pradesh. The study further shows that 55 per cent of the total child workers of these establishments belong to the places falling outside the Himanchal Pradesh. It is interesting to note that no child belongs to the neighboring states of Punjab, Haryana, Jammu & Kashmir and Uttar Pradesh. Table 7 gives the detail of place of origin.

Table 7

Sr. No.	Name of Place	No. of Children	Percentage
1	2	3	4
1.	Shimla	11	13.75

2.	Solan	11	13.75
3.	Mandi	4	5.00
4.	Hamirpur	2	2.50
5.	Kullu	1	1.25
6.	Una	1	1.25
7.	Sirmaur	4	5.00
8.	Kangra	2	2.50
9.	Bihar	10	12.50
10.	Nepal	34	42.50

Table 8 deals with the nature of leave allowed by owners of these establishments to the child workers. 70 per cent of the total child workers have stated that no leave is allowed to them in any shape. However, one child worker has mentioned that his employer has allowed him 10 days as the leave period with full pay, 13.75 per cent of child workers have mentioned that they are given 12 days as a leave period with full benefits annually. 4 child workers have stated that they avail annually 15 days as a leave period and get full wages for these days 2 workers out of 80 child workers have written in their response that they avail 24 days as leave period and their owners make full payment for the above said days also, 3.75 per cent of the child workers of the sample units have mentioned 36 days as the leave period with full wages as agreed to by their owners. However, serial number 7 of Table 8 reveals that 3 child workers get days leave annually.

Table 8 : Detail of Leave Availed by Child Workers

Sr. No.	Annually leave	No. of Children	Percentage
1	2	3	4
1.	No leave	56	70
2.	10 days	1	1.25
3.	12 days	11	13.75
4.	15 days	4	5.0
5.	24 days	2	2.5
6.	36 days	3	3.75
7.	52 days	3	3.75

The clothing facilities availed by the child workers is depicted in Table 9. It is revealed that 48 children, that is 60 per cent of the total sample children interviewed, have mentioned that they do not avail the clothing facilities of interviewed have stated that they are given clothes by their employers in lieu of their wages. Besides, 12.5 per cent child workers have stated that they are given old clothes by their owners.

Table 9 : Detail of Clothing Facilities Availed

Sr. No.	Provision of Cloth	No. of Children	Percentage
1	2	3	4
1.	No provision	48	60
2.	Old clothes	10	12.5
3.	Yes	22	27.5

The study also shows that all the child workers interviewed by the author get the food and housing facilities. They have also mentioned that no recovery is made by their employers from their wages even if some breakage is done by them incidentally or accidentally. They are also provided electricity facilities and water facilities for taking bath and washing clothes.

Similarly, the data collected and tabulated under Table 10 speaks about the mode of entertainment provided to the child workers in these establishments. 58.75 per cent of the child workers have mentioned that there are not entertainment facilities to them. However, 25.0 per cent child workers have stated that they get entertainment through radio and tapes and 15 per cent have mentioned that they are given facilities of television by their employers. The child workers have made clear in their statements that they can reap the benefit of entertainment facilities only in the late hours of the evening and night when there is no rush of work for want of the customers.

Table 10 : Detail of Entertainment Facilities of Child Workers

Sr.No.	Made of Entertainment	No. of Children	Percentage
1	2	3	4
1.	No provision	47	58.75
2.	Radio	11	13.75
3.	Tape	10	12.5
4.	Television	12	15.0

So far as nature of their duties is concerned, they are: washing of utensils, preparation of tea and sweets, cleaning of table and chairs, sweeping of room, etc. Despite of large number in these establishments, they are not covered by any law or regulation and they are supposed to carry out jobs of mixed nature.

Table 11 : Detail of the Working Hours of the Children

Sr. No.	Working Hours	No. of Children	Percentage
1	2	3	4
1.	0-8	0.00	0.00
2.	8-12	12	15.00
3.	12-15	58	72.5
4.	Above 15	10	12.5

It is also evident from the statements of the child workers, that they are to work without intermittent rest pauses from morning till evening. It is revealed from the study of Table 11 all the child workers are to toil between 8-15 hours without any rest. 15 per cent of the total child workers have stated that they work for 8-12 hours a day, 72.5 per cent child workers have stated that their working hours vary between 12-15 hours, and 10 child workers, i.e. 12.5 per cent have mentioned that they are to work tirelessly for 15 hours or above every day. It is generally found from the statement made by child workers that their employers do not follow any child labour welfare legislation. As the child workers are whole-time servants and live in the premises provided by their employers, they usually work from early hours of the morning to late hours in the night without taking any rest.

CONCLUSION

The data collected in the present survey presents a clear-cut picture of the working conditions of the child workers in the tea-stalls, sweet-shops and dhabas located in the periphery of Shimla City. The survey has shown that 37.83 per cent are still the child workers carrying out different types of occupations in these establishments. Out of 212 total employees in these establishments, 80 are child workers belonging to different castes. About 68.75 per cent child workers belong to Rajput families, 20 per cent are the Brahmins and 8 per cent fall in the category of the scheduled castes and scheduled tribes. There is only 1.25 per cent child workers who belong to the Muslim community.

The child workers have stated to have got the occupation through three different modes, viz., self, through relationship and other sources. It is seen from the survey that 25 per cent child workers got their occupations by their individual initiatives, 45 per cent through the media of their relationships, and 30 per cent could get their employment through other sources. The main reason for joining the occupation by these child workers is stated as "poverty." It may be observed that caste has played a little role in th social evil of child labour. It is the poverty which seems to have been responsible to generate the evil of child labour in each and every establishment of country.

The survey has shown beyond the shadow of doubt that the working conditions of the children are far from satisfaction. The survey results reveal that the owners of these establishments do not adhere to laws made to regulate the hours of work as prescribed under the Child Labour (Prohibition and Regulation) Act, 1986. It has been observed that the daily working hours of children vary between 8 to 15 hours, as against 6 hours prescribed under Section 7, Clause (3) of the Child Labour (P & R) Act, 1986. To the surprise of the authors, 10 child workers have stated that they are forced to work even for more than 15 hours a day without any rest. The data collected reveals that the child workers are not allowed any rest during the whole course of their work in a day. Almost all the child workers interviewed have mentioned that there is no specific period given to them for the purpose of rest. This practice is highly in contravention to Section 7(3) of the Child Labour (P & R) Act, 1986, wherein every employer is under statutory obligation to arrange the period of work on each day in such a manner that no for more than 3 hours before he had interval for rest for at least one hour. It is also observed while the interview of the child workers that they are to work even in the late hours of the evening and there is no bar on the employers to restrain them as the employment of the children between 7 P.M. and 8 P.M. is totally prohibited under clause 4 of section 7 of the Act.

It is also quite evident that the child workers do not get any weekly holidays. 70 per cent of the children interviewed have stated that they are not entitled to any kind of leave. Only 30 per cent of the sampled units have mentioned that they get annual leave ranging between 10 to 52 days. The survey results, therefore, show that the mandate of Section 8 of the Child Labour (P & R) Act, 1986, is not at all obeyed by the owners of tea-stalls, sweet-shops and dhabas.

So far as the health provision are concerned, the survey shows that the owners provide tot he child workers a nominal type of medical facilities in case of their illness. All the 80 interviewed child workers have stated that they are provided with the house facilities, drinking water facilities, lighting facilities, etc. by their employers. However, it is generally observed from the study that they are poorly paid and even get their wages between a poor range of rupees 0-350. 97.5 per cent of the total child workers have stated that they get their wage between Rs. 0-350.. There are only 2 children who have mentioned their wages above Rs. 350 per month. The survey, therefore, discloses that the poor child workers are not paid even the minimum wages by their employers which is sheerly in contravention to the decision of the Supreme Court given in M.C. Mehta vs. State of Tamil Nadu (AIR 1991 SC 417). The Honorable Court in this case has held that the child workers must get at least minimum wages which comes to 60 per cent of prescribed minimum wage for adult employees doing same job to be given to child in view of special adaptability of child's tender age to such work.

It is also observed from the survey that the educational profile of the child workers is very poor. None has stated his education above eighth standard. 45 per cent of the child workers have been found totally illiterate and there are only 55 per cent of the child workers whose education various between 5th-8th standards. It is observed that the majority of child workers have joined these occupations because they are basically poor and need wages as a source of their livelihood. There are hardly any night school for those who want to continue their studies. It is also revealed that there is lack of appreciation on the part of their employers to give them education while serving in their establishments. The findings of the study therefore go against the spirit of the decision of the Supreme Court in M.C. Mehta v. State of Tamil Nadu.

It is also equally clear that extreme poverty is the main reason for the wide prevalence of child labour. In Annexure-III, 79 child workers out of 80 have stated poverty as a reason for joining the establishments. Thus, it is revealed from the that child labour could not be weeded out despite several welfare legislations enacted by the Government from time-to time. It needs a change in social attitude. Social awareness is also needed to discourage the practice of child labour. Besides this, the tightening of laws and activising enforcement machinery are needed badly to weed out the child labour in its true perspective.

3

Child Labour in Chikan Industry

Chikan Industry is a totally home-based industry. It has been seen that the Chikan embroidery is basically done at home by the female member of the household. Because of the strict purdah system observed in the families which are predominantly muslims, none of the female chikan workers gets out of his/her house and consequently know little about the outside world. As a result of this, the employers exploit these workers extensively and pay them very low wages. This accrues a very large profit for the employers and also middlemen are able to make a neat sum of money.

Summarily it can be said that the unorganised nature of the Chikan Industry leaves a lot of room for exploitation of the workers by the employers and the middlemen. Thus, there is a need to organise these women and children workers, supported by legislations regarding minimum wages and honourable working conditions.

The home-based workers should be brought under the purview of various Labour Laws. The legislators, administrators and social workers should bear in mind that amelioration of the socio-economic condition of these home based workers should be accorded top most priority while enacting or implementing any legislation for regulating the working and living conditions of Chikan Workers.

The National Commission on labour has not been able to define this 'unorganised sector' but describes it as an assignment of conditions which have not helped organisation in present economic objective because of certain constraints such as the following:

(a) Casual nature employment,
(b) Ignorance and Illiteracy,
(c) Small size of establishment with low capital investment per person employed,
(d) Scattered nature of establishments,
(e) Superior strength of the employers operating singularly or in combination.

The Commission has also given the types of child workers who have been engaged in the unorganised sector. These types are the following:

1. Contract Labour including constitution workers.
2. Casual Labour.
3. Labour employed in small scale industry.
4. Handloom/Powerloom Industry.
5. Bidi and Cigar workers.
6. Employees in shops and commercial establishments.
7. Sweepers and scavengers.
8. Workers in tanneries.
9. Tribal labour.
10. Other improtected labour.

The illustration noted above points out that the Chikan Industry has all the characteristics of an unorganised industry. Most of the workers that are employed there-whether they are adults or children, man or women-are found completely illiterate and ignorant and also there is low capital per investment per work. The workers are always exploited. Thus we can safely assume that the Chikan Industry should be placed under the unorganised Sector or industries employing child workers.

It has been seen that "Chikan" embroidery is just like a shining feather in the artistic cap of Lucknow.

The art of Chikan Embroidery was mostly confined within the walls of old localities of Luckonw but later on, it stretched within a radius of about 100 km from North to South, West to East of Lucknow. About 50,000 to 60,000 people are engaged in this art and it has become a profession of the members of the Muslim families and it is passing from generation to generation.

Saleha Khatoon

(Recipient of National Award) Development Training Centre, Government of India, 482/24, Nai Basti, Iradat Nagar, Daliganj, Lucknow.

Even Saleha Khatoon belongs to the traditional family where chikan Embroidery is in the blood. One of her table covers was chosen for National Award in 1982. After that she got aid from the Government and opened a Training Centre for children in her house only in 1983 but due to insufficient aid from Government she had to close down the centre in 1987. Now all the workers are engaged in their respective homes and get the orders from-

UPICA HANDICRAFTS,

89, Crowngate Chowk,

Lucknow.

From the area of Daliganj, 50 children were selected from amongst who were working in their homes.

Sex Composition

The following Table shows the sex-wise distribution of respondents in the sample selected for study.

Table 1: Showing sex composition of the respodents

Sex	No. of respondents	Percentage
Males	2	4
Females	48	96
Total	50	100

The Table shows that 96 per cent of the respondents are females. It proves that embroidery is basically done by females who do a better job than males and it does not usually attract males as the Zardoji industry does because of low wages.

Generally girls only do this because they are not allowed to go out of the house after they cross certain age and they have to observe purdah because of their Muslim background their parents feel that if the girls are going to stay at home, they must do some job to contribute to the family income.

Age Composition

While selecting the children for survey, the only consideration was that the child selected for the survey should be below the age of fourteen years as per the definition of the child given by the Child Labour (Prohibition and Regulation) Act 1986.

The following Table shows the age of 50 children surveyed in Daliganj.

Table 2: Showing Age, composition of the Respondents

Age (Years)	No. of Respondents	Percentage
6-8	2	4
8-10	10	20
10-12	21	42
12-14	17	34
Total	50	100

The above table reveals that the majority of the children belongs to the age groups of 10-12 years, followed by 12-14, 8-10 and 6-8 in that order.

The average age of starting work has been 8.57 years. 'Gangrade' has also maintained that "the usual age of entry into employment seems to be 8-10 years..."

Religion of the Respondents

The Table 3 shows religion of the child workers because it plays a prominent role in shaping the outlook of life in later yeras.

Table: 3 Showing religion of respondents family

Religion	No. of Children	Percentage
Hindus	--	--
Muslim	50	100

Above the Table shows that all the respondents were Muslims and it only proves that Muslims still preserve the art of Chikan Work.

Reasons behind taking up Chikan Work

It has been found that generally Chikan Work was the traditional occupation of the family. 50 children came into this field because of the encouragement provided by their parents or other close relatives.

The families which were selected in the sample were affiliated with UPICA Handicrafts. The head of the family had enrolled his/her name at the office at 'Crowngate' and got the pieces to be embroidered at their residence. Conveniently Tuesday has been a fixed day when they had to take the complete work deposit it there and get the new orders.

Table 4: Persons who encouraged the respondents in Chikan Work

Persons who brought them in Chikan Work	No. of Respondents	Percentage
Parents	45	90
Other relatives	5	10
Total	50	100

The Table 4 unreavels that 90% of the respondents were encouraged by their parents to come into the Chikan Work.

Reasons for taking up Chikan Work

The following table shwos the reasons due to which the respondents worked.

Table 5: Showing reasons for respondents taking up the Chikan Work

Reasons for doing Work	No. of Children	Percentage
Family tradition	40	80
For earning	9	18
Hobby	1	2
Total	50	100

The above Table shows that it has been due to family tradition that 80% respondents have been working. The number of children coming in the Chikan Work for earning themselves and as part of their hobby been quite low.

Table 6: Showing the training aspects of the respondents

Whether trained	No. of respondents	Percentage
Yes	5	10
No	45	90
Total	50	100

Training

The Table 6 shows the percentage of trained and untrained and workers.

The Table 6 makes it clear that the majority (90%) of the respondents are untrained. Only 10 per cent of them were trained in Chikan Work.

Table 7: Showing training in relation to age

Whether untruined	Age Groups 6-8	8-10	10-12	12-14	No. of respondents
Yes	--	--	2	3	5
No	2	10	19	14	45
Total	2	10	21	17	50

The above Table unreavels that children who were trained generally belonged to a higher age group (i.e. 12-14). Among the untrained children the highest percentage came from 10-12 age group, followed by 12-14, 8-10 and 6-8.

Duration of Work

The following table gives the time span for which these children have been engaged in the work.

The Table 8 shows that 76 per cent of them have been working for more than 1 year. 20% of them have been doing this work for six months and 4% of them had recently joined this trade.

Table 8: Showing duration of engagement in the work

Time upon engaged in this work	Number of respondents	Percentage
For more than 1 year	38	76
Between 6 months and 1 year	10	20
For less than 6 month	2	4
Total	50	100

SUMMARY

1. The majority of children in this trade has been the females.

2. The highest number of children doing the Chikan Work has been found to be in 12-14 age groups.

3. All the respondents have been from Muslim families.

4. Overwhelming majority of the cases have been encouraged by their parents to join the Chikan Work.

5. Keeping up the family tradition has been the general reson behind the respondent's coming for Chikan Work.

6. Only a lesser number of children are trained for the Chikan Work.

7. The majority of respondents have been in the Chikan Work for more than one year.

FAMILY PROFILE OF CHILD WORKERS

Family is the main institution in shaping the child's personality. Therefore the form and character of the family is of utmost importance for developing the child's personality.

It has been seen that the form of the family is greatly affected by the social and economic changes that have taken place in recent years but the basic biological and social needs which guide the essential functions of the family have not yet changed. Though some of the original functions of the family such as the educational, recreational and religious have been taken over by other social agencies get its basic function which centres around the bio-psycho and social needs of man have not been affected.

The importance of the family has been rightly summed up by Mciver and Page in these words-

"...of all the organisations, large or small which society unfolds none transcend the family in the intensity of its sociological society."

The Psychological and environmental influence of the family on the child is so deep and takes place so rapidly that Psychologists say that the child acquires all the traits of his personality and charcter of his adulthood before he attains the age of 5 and in some cases even earlier. Since the family forms such an integral part of the child's life, it is essential to study the family background of the child.

It was found during the survey that the average size of the family was large. The main reason was that they had the view-point that family planning was prohibited by Islam and they also believed that they needed extra hands to earn and contribute in the family income. Unfortunately they could not understand the underlying fact that large size of families means that there are extra mouths to feed and bodies to clothe. Consequently a large number of children are found in the families which were selected for the study.

Table 9: Showing sex composition of respondents families

Composition	Total number of family members	Percentage N=500 (100%)
Male	220	44%
Female	280	56%
Total	500	100%

From the total 50 families surveyed the average size of

the family is 10-0 where as the desired size of family members is 3.8 by 2000 AD. The breakup being 220 male members or 280 females.

The present survey has revealed that as many as 280 number of siblings have been found in the sampled families. The following Table has given the breakup of the families according to the number of siblings therein.

Table 10: Showing siblings of the family

Number of siblings	Number of families	Percentage
1 child	--	--
2-3 children	8	16
4-5 Children	10	20
6-7 children	20	40
7 and above	12	24
Total	50	100

The Table 10 shows that the highest number of families were having the 6-7 number of siblings, followed by the families having 7 or above number of siblings, 4-5 number of siblings and 2-3 number of siblings in the order. The average number of siblings per family was 5-6.

Table 11: Showing literacy/illiteracy of father

Education of father	Number of children	Percentage N=47 (100%)
Yes	12	25%
No	35	74%
Total	47	99%

It is stated that one of the major causes of child labour is said to be illiteracy and ignorance of parents. This leads to a lack of appreciation of education on the parts of the parents and also limits the outlook towards life. Such parental handicapes are at once reflected in the child as it is primarily in the family that the early socialization of the child takes place.

Table 12: Showing literacy/illiteracy of mother

Education of mother	Number of children	Percentage
Yes	5	10
No	45	90
Total	50	100

The Tables 11 and 12 show the educational status of the parents (father and mother separately) of children studies in this research, employed in the Chikan Industry.

It is seen from the Table 11 that 24% of the children's fathers was educated and 70% of the children's father was not educated. Six percent of the children had lost their father.

The Table 12 shows that out of 50 children 10% of their mothers was educated, and 90% of their mothers was uneducated. In comparison, educational status of fathers was better than mothers. Yet the overall educational status of both the parents was far from satisfactory. In the families where both the parents are illiterate, children are bound to be called upon to take up some job or occupation to contribute to the income of the family.

Table 13: Showing the occupation of the head of the family

Occupation of the Head of family	Number of families	Percentage N= 47 (100%)
1. Government servant	3	6.38
2. Hawker	8	17.02
3. Vegetable vendors	6	12.76
4. Cycle repair shopworker	8	17.02
5. Rickshaw puller	8	17.02
6. Factory worker	8	17.02
7. Causual labourer	6	12.76
Total	47	99.98

Numerous studies, have brought to light the crucial role the mother plays in the development of the child. And if the mother follows the Purdah system and if she is uneducated, she becomes economically and psychologically dependent and socially backward. She is hardly capable of bringing up her children as healthy boys and girls and well adjusted adults. It is important to determine the occupation of the head of the family as it has an impact upon the children's job, work or economic activity.

The Table 13 contains the information regarding the parent's occupation. It reveals that though the occupation of the head of the household varied yet the most common occupation was that of hawker (16%), Rickshaw puller (16%) and factory worker (16%). Only in 3% of the cases the childre's father was a Government employee and 12% was vegetable vendors and 12% was casual labourers.

Most of the heads of households are employed in occupation requiring little or no skill. Most of them work in the unorganized sector. Unorganized sector has been defined as that sector which has not been able to organise itself in pursuit of common objectives. Casual nature of employment, ignorance and illiteracy on the part of the workers, small size and scattered nature of establishments and superior strength of employers, are some of the characterstics, of unorganized occupations. There is also little security of employment or assurance of a stable income in these occupations. Under such circumstances parents have little choice but to send their children to work.

It is immense importance to determine the family income. Since one of the major causes of child labour is the low income of the family and the general poor economic condition. The family income comprises of the income of the head of the household, and income of the earning dependents, that is of wife and children or of any other person in the family.

The unwillingness on the part of family members to

disclose the actual income has left a wide margin of error. We relied on observation about the standard of living and also on the secondary services to give us an estimate about the family income. The follwing Table shows family income (monthly).

Table 14: Showing Family Income of the Respondents family

Family income monthly (in Rs.)	Number of families	Percentage
0-200	4	8
200-400	10	20
400-600	11	22
600-800	6	12
800-1000	19	38
1000 and above	--	--
Total	50	100

It is revealed from the above Table that out of total number of families, 8% had family income less than Rs. 200/- per month, 20% had family income between 200-400, 22% from 400-600, 12% from 600-800 and 38% above per month.

It is evident from the above Table that the standard of living was poor. In these families the income could be supplemented by the efforts of extra earning members-the wife and children who were engaged in home based industry, like Chikan, Mukesh and Zardozi industries. Low income compelled the parents to send their children to work in the above said industries.

After seeing the children involved in the Chikan work one is likely to assume that the Chikan craft is handed over from generation to generation and in this case it becomes the family occupation. Thus an information with regard to the number of family members engaging in this work (Chikan) was gathered in this study. The following Table shows the number of family members engaged in Chikan craft besides the children interviwed in the study.

Table 15: Showing the number of persons of the family engaged in Chikan Work

Number of persons of the family	Number of families engaged in Chikan Work	Percentage
1-2	19	38
3-4	17	34
5-6	12	24
7 and above	2	4
Total	50	100

From the above Table it is evident that most of the families have two or more members engaged in the Chikan craft while the highest percent of families were engaging between one and two family members in this work the number of families engaging between 3 and 6 members was substantially high.

38 percent of the families had 2 members while 17 families or 34% had 3-4members engaged in Chikan craft. Another 12 families or 24% had 5-6 members in the Chikan craft and only 2 or 4% had more than 7 members in Chikan work.

SUMMARY

1. The average size of the respondent's family members is 10.00 (per family).

2. The average number of siblings of the respondents families has been 5.6 (per family).

3. The percent of respondent's father being illiterate was predominatly high.

4. Ninety percent of the respondent's mother was also illiterate.

5. Most of heads of the households were casually employed persons.

6. None of the families surveyed had the income above Rs. one

thousand per month.

7. The number of family members engaging in the Chikan work, besides the children interviewed, was quite high.

EDUCATIONAL DETERMINANT OF CHILD WORKERS

Education had been defined as the "Art of developing and cultivating physical, intellectual, aesthetic and moral faculties of the individual with a view to enabling him to respond positively to demands and responsibilities of his social being.

In all developing countries including India, there is no lack awarness of the importance of education, primary, secondary, intermediate and higher nor any shortage of commitment to achieving the educated society, But there are many constraints which come in the way of achieving the coveted goal. These are poverty, low status of women and consequent neglect of girls education, child marriage, chornic shortage of buildings and equipment, and defective supervision and administration in the field of education. These factors people's participation and development.

The Directive Principles of State Policy of the Indian Constitution (Article 45) include the following :

"The State shall endeavour to provide within ten years of the commencent of the Constitution free and compulsory education, for all children upto the age of 14 years".

Although the Indian Constitution has been in existence for more than 4 decades, the literacy percentage in the country as not gone up beyond 35 percent, The literacy among the women and the scheduled castes, tribe population is more depressing. Thus, time stipulate in the Constitution has been extended several times to wipe out illiteracy and ignorance from the Indian scene. The educational system in India was devised not for universal learning, but to produce small number of clerks and junior officials needed to run the status-quo administration during the British rule.

The United Nations Declaration of Rights of the child has emphasized the importance of education in the life of a child in these words:

"Education is an essential need of the child especifically the kind of education that will help him to develop the knowledge judgement, and social and moral values to play his proper role in society when he becomes an adult".

Thus, in fufilment of this constitution no child should be allowed to work on the street, or in other places of employment. The child should indeally be attending school to grow into a responsible adult. But this is not to be; the following table attempts to show how many of the children in Dalilganj area have been to school? How many of them have dropped out and how many have never been to school?

Table 16: Showing distribution of children according to status of their Schooling

Status of Schooling	Number of children	Percentage
Currently attending school	5	10
Had attended School	19	38
Never attended school	26	5
Total	50	100

Looking at the Table it can be found that there was only 10% of 50 children who were currently attending school. Thirty eight percent of the children had dropped out of school while a large percentage i.e. 52% of the children had never been to school.

By speaking to the mothers of children employed on the Chikan craft, we discovered that although they were aware of the importance of education their girls, they could not send their girls to schools, because of various constraints and pressures of poverty. The table 16 gives information with regard to the present state of children's (interviewed) schooling.

Table 17: Showing the present level of standard of education

Classes	Number of children	Percentage
I	1	20
II	1	20
III	1	20
IV	--	--
V	2	40
Total	5	100

The Table 17 revealed that there were only five children who were attending the schools presently. Out of the children attending the schools two were in the class Vth whereas the other three children were in equally divided in classes Ist, IInd and IIIrd.

The following Table provides information with regard to the type of school (whether private or public) being attended by children presently :

Table 18: Showing type of school being attended by the children

Typology	Number of Students	Percentage
Private (Semi)	1	20
Public	4	80
Total	5	100

The Table 18 revealed that the higher percentage of children attending the school presently were in public schools, only one out of five children was found to be in a private School.

The Table 19 contains information regarding the question who supported their schooling :

Table 19: Showing who supports their education

Person supporting	Number of Students	Percentage
Father	2	40
Mother	1	20
Other relatives		
(Elder brother)	1	20
By himself	1	20

The Table 19 revealed that the majority of the cases the children's schooling was supported by either of the parents, father in two cases and the mother in one case, out of the total number of five children attending schools presently However, in one case the child was supporting his schooling by himself.

Discussion

The Table 16 has revealed that as many as 52 percent of the children interviewed had never been to Schools.

On speaking to the mothers of children employed in the Chikan craft, it was discovered that although they were aware of the importance of educating their girls, they could not send their girls to shcools, because of various reasons. Poverty was the main cause for not sending the children to the schools. They could not afford educating their children.

Regarding school drop-outs, the most important reason was stated to be that all girls belonged to the Muslim community where there was a very strict purdah system. The girls on attaining the age of puberty were made to observe purdah strictly. And thus the parents kept their girls at home rather than send them to schools. These parents preferred earning on the part of these girls rather than allowing them to sit idile at home.

SUMMARY

The picture obtaining with regard to the educational standard of the children interviewed was very depressing with the state of affairs regarding the educational background of the children. One must look at the government policies already existing with regard to the education of children. One easily discovers that there is an emphasis an the education of girls, vocationalization of secondary education and free and compulsory education for all children under 14 years.

Thus it is abundantly clear that although the Government is giving due importance to education by including it in the Five Year Plans, a lot still needs to be done in this field.

HEALTH DEPARTMENT OF CHILD WORKERS

It is fairly established that health of any nation depands upon the health status of its population especially that of the younger generation. But it is amazing that in India even after forty years of endependence, the overall health and nutritional situations continue to be bad. Although India has made tremendous progress in all other spheres of life like industry, science and technology, space and so on, the sphere of health seems totally neglected. It will be clear by the following figures:

(1) The infant mortality rate is 125 to 1000 whereas in developed countries it is 10-14 to 1000.

(2) Life expectancy at birth is 54-5 years as compared to 75 years in developed countries.

(3) 36% of school children are malnourished.

But now the efforts are being made to improve the standard of health of the population through a nationwide programme of immunization under Integrated Child Development Scheme (I.C.D.S). In evaluating the health condition of the children, one of the major constraints was that there was no possibility of any clinical examination and no records were available to substanitiate the information collected with regard to the death of the childre. The limited response and the ability of the respondents to communicate gave us some picutre about the prevailing health situation of the children employed in the Chikan Industry.

The factors affecting the health of the children are of two kinds. First, there are the health problems to which the children are exposed because of the fact that they are required to work for long hours without rest. Secondly, the children are also exposed to certain environmental, social, biological factors together with the poor economic conditions prevailing in these families.

Looking at the occupational health hazards because the child while doing Chikan work sits in a small poorly lit and ventilated homes in crowded mohallas, which provides him both the workplace and living space.

Sitting in the pasture of cross legged or with leges outstretched with their bodies bent slightly forward on floors and working for such long periods results in backaches and due to poorly lit rooms, it damages the eye of the child.

The following Table shows the diseases from which the children are suffering.

Table 20: Showing various ailments of working children

Ailments	Number of Children N=50	Percentage
1. Eyes water often	37	74
2. Headache	36	72
3. Backaches	42	84
4. Pain in the arms	3162	
5. Giddiness	17	34
6. Pain in joints	10	20

The Table 20 shows that 84% respondents complained about their backache, 74% complained about their eyesight problems, followed by 72% complaining about headache, 62% about pain in arms, 34% giddiness and 20% pain in joints.

It must be noted that a child often complained of more than one ailment. Thus a child had headache, backache, or pain in the arms.

The next inevitable questions are whether or not any treatment is undertaken for the above mentioned ailments and if any treatment is undertaken then where has it been taken, in government hospitals, private practitioners or any other place?

The following Tables 21 and 23 provide information on the above two questions:

Table 21: Showing whether or not treatment was obtained

Nature of response	Number of response	Percentage
Yes	6	12
No	44	88
Total	50	100

It is found from the above Table that the majority of the children (88 percent) did dot take any treatment, while the rest i.e., 12 percent consulted some physician for their ailment. The findings of this table further proves that the families where Chikan work is taken as a source of employment often suffer from poor economic condition which does not allow them to incur any expenditure on health problems.

Table 23: Showing the type of treatment undertaken by respondents

Type of treatment	Number of respondents	Percentage N=6=100%

Government Hospital	2	33
Private practitioner1	16	
Quacks treatment	3	50
Total	6	99

The following Table deals with question which place was consulted by the respondents for treatment of ailments.

The above Table shows that the highest percentage of respondents consulted the quacks for their treatment follwed practitioners in the sequential order.

The next question which was asked pertaining to the health of the child was whether or not the child has been vaccinated in his/her childhood. Since the child was unable to answer the question the mother was asked this question.

Table 24: Showing the status of vaccination and immunization

Nature of response	Number of response	Percentage
Yes	5	10
No	45	90
Total	50	100

It is found from the above table that only 10% had been inoculated whereas the rest 90% had not received any incoulation.

It should be noted of the 10 percent who were vaccinated none of their mothers could specify the exact names of the vaccinations given to their children. During the discussion it was found that some of the vaccinations like D.T.P. and Polio which required administration of three doses in specified period of time, could not be given in their full doses.

SUMMARY

To sum up, it can be said that general public is quite indifferent and apathetic towards immunization. The main cause of this apathy is the lack of awareness and information regarding the benefits of immunization on people's part.

It has also been found that if the child develops minor reactions such as burning fever etc. after getting inoculated, the parents develop aversion towards inoculation. They refuse to get their children inoculated in future.

Another cause for general apathy towards inoculation is that male members of the family never find time to take the child to hospitals for inoculation or to acquire awareness and knowledge about the benefits of immunization. The need. therefore, is to spread the general awareness on the part of general public regarding various inoculations and immunizations.

NUTRITIONAL AND DIETARY DERTERMINANT OF CHILD WORKERS

Nutrition is an important factor in building up of the health of a nation and malnutrition is a very serious problem of developing countries. The most severely and chronically malnourished are the poor, specially the infants, children and mothers. Nutritional status affects health, labour productivity, learning capacity and their income. Malnutrition leads to deficiency and acts as a major cause of impairment in the proper growth of the children and women specially in the rural areas. In fact malnutrition makes a particular class of people a vulnerable class.

We shall attempt to study the nutritional level of the children employed in the Chikan Industry. Since the children doing Chikan Work are girls, their nutritional standard is very poor. The main criteria for judging the nutritional level was height, weight, protein and calories intake. However due to absence of specialised knowledge in this field only an estimate could be made of the nutritional level of the children through observation.

The Table 25 shows that only 40% of the responent seemed to be nourished. The Table 25 shows that majority of the respondents were sufferring from nutritional deficiency. Only 40 percent of the respondents was stated to be healthy whereas the rest 60 percent were nutritionally deficient children.

Table 25: Showing the state of nutrition among the Child Workers

Sate of nutrition	Number of child workers	Percentage
Malnourished	30	60
Healthy	20	40
Total	50	100

Table 26: Showing state of diet among the Child Workers

Opinion	Number of respondents	Percentage
Getting enough to eat with good quality	2	4
Not getting enough/the quality food to eat	23	46
Unable to Answer	25	50

The information with regard to the respondents diet was collected. It is being presented in Table 26.

The Table 26 shows that the 46 per cent respondents were dissatisfied with the diet and its quality and only 4 per cent were satisfied with the diet and its quality.

It is noticeable that exactly half of the respondents (50 per cent) could not provide any definite answer with regard to the diet and its quality.

The next question was regarding the type of food being taken through the day by the respondents.

It is found that in the breakfast only 40 percent of the workeres ate fresh cooked food while 42 per cent had often left overs to eat and 18 per cent bought biscuits or somosa, etc. from the market. The Table 27 also points out that for lunch only 20 percent of the child workers ate fresh cooked food while 76 percent had leftovers to eat and 21 percent of the child workers bought puri, etc. from the market.

Table 27: Showing the type of food taken at different points of time in the day by the respondents

Type of food	Breakfast %	Lunch %	Dinner %
Whether fresh cooked	20 40	10 20	15 30
Whether left overs	21 42	38 76	34 68
Whether brought from market	9 18	2 4	1 2
Total	50 100	50 100	50 100

The general finding from the Table 27 only substantiates that the quality of the food had been far from satisfactory. It had low nutritional value. Most of the child workers either ate the left-overs or bought food from the market to satisfy power being poor they could not have bought enough and quality food from the market.

SUMMARY

(1) The health of the majority of the child workers had been very poor.

(2) Among the child workers who provided answer regarding the question as to their diet and its quality, it was found that the majority were deprived of their full diet and also the quality of food was poor.

(3) The vast majority of child workers either depended on the left-over food or the food bought from the market.

WORKING CONDITIONS OF CHILD WORKERS

It has been fairly established that complete abolition of child labour in any underdeveloped society is not practicable. Child labour has come to stay in our societies as a necessary evil. In fact, child labour continues as long as there is poverty in any society. Though we have made so many laws banning it, yet it won't be of much use as people much satisfy their basic wants and when their income is so meagre they will ask their children to work and supplement the family income. Thus a ban child labour will neither be feasible nor practical.

The working condition of children employed in India are absolutely inhuman. The ILO categorically states-

"The child's creativeness and ability to transcend reality are blurted and his whole mental world in improved."

Despite the fact that the Constitution has been in existence for the last forty years the working conditions of children in various occupations continue to be inhuman. It was felt that since a complete ban on child labour was not practical nor feasible, the working conditions under which children worked could be regulated.

The child labour (Prohibition & Regulation) Act 1986 was promulgated with a view to regulate the working conditions of child labour. Although this Act is a step in the right direction, it is very difficult to enforce it in a country which is poor and over populated. The appaling working conditions under which children are forced to work makes a mockery of Article 24 of the Directive Principles of Sate Policy which states-

"No child below the age of 14 years shall be employed in any factory or mine or enganged in any other hazardous employment."

Although girls constitute a large percentage of child labour, they are mainly engaged in home-based work. The Act makes no mention of the home-based category of child labour. Because of this short coming it is very difficult to regulate working conditions of children working at home.

Hours of Work

The following Table contains the information regarding the working hours of child workers engaged in Chikan Industry.

Table 28: Showing relationship between child workers and the hours of work

Working hours (daily)	Number of child worker	Percentage
Upto 2 hours	5	10
2-4 hours	13	26 64
4-6 hours	14	28
6-8 hours	17	34
8 to 10 hours	1	2

The above Table shows that 64% of the child workers were working for less than 6 hours a day (in accordance with provisions of the Act). These children usually take a break in between the working hours to do some other work in the house. A few of the girls also go to school that is why they work for about six hours. It has been generally observed that the female child workers work for lesser hours because they have to do household course like cooking and sewing clothes and also as the baby sister. It is also noteworthy that about 34% of the child workers were working for more than six hours a day.

Duration of Employment

The information regarding the duration of Chikan work by the child workers was also collected and the same is being presented in the Table 29.

The Table 29 shows the duration of employment of the children. A large percentage of the children started work at a very young age and hence had been working for more than 5 years or so. The highest percent of child workers (28) had been found to be working for between 5 and 6 years, followed by 22 per cent for 3-4 years, 20 per cent for 2-3 years.

Table 29: Showing the distribution of child workers according their duration of chikan work

Duration of the Chikan Work	Number of child worker	Percentage
Less than 3 months	1	2
6 months-1 years	1	2
1-2 years	10	20
2-3 years	10	20
3-5 years	11	22
5-6 years	14	28
6 years and above	3	9
Total	50	100

Table 30: Showing the distribution of child workers according to length of Chikan workers and number of working hours

No. of working hours Upto	2	2-4	4-6	6-8	8-10
Less than 3 months	1	--	--	--	--
6 months -1 year	1	--	--	--	--
1-2 years	2	5	2	1	--
2-3 years	1	5	4	--	--
3-5 years	--	2	5	4	--
5-6 years	--	1	2	11	--
6 years and above	--	--	--	2	1
Total	5	13	13	18	1

It has been observed that the working hours increased as the duration of employment increases. Thus the Table 30 attempts to show a relationship between length of time employed and number of working hours per day of the working children.

It has been also observed that if a girl was employed for more than 5 years, her working hours decreased. This is because of the fact that as they grow older they have to help more in the household course and also look after the younger siblings of the house.

Distribution of Children According to Place of Work

We attempted to study the distribution of child workers according to their place of work, Although the children are found to be mostly working at home, some of them are found to be working at different places other than that of their homes.

The following Table shows the distribution of children according to their place of work.

Table 31: Showing the distribution of child workers according to their place of work

Place of work	Number of children	Percentage
At home	34	68
At neighbours	16	32
Total	50	100

Thus, it is clear from the Table 31 that 32% of child workers worked at neighbour's house. These neighbours get pieces of work which require different stitches. Since not every girl child worker knew stitching work of chikan, different girls work at the same piece. However, the mothers of the child workers were found to be working at their homes only. It has been observed that the working conditions prevalent are found to be lacking in several basic amenities. Thus the following table contains the information whether the working place had the basic necessary conditions of work.

Table 32

Items	Satisfactory	Percentage	Poor	Percentage
Cleanliness	18	36	32	64
Ventilation	23	46	27	54

Lighting	23	46	27	54

It is apparent from the above Table that very few households had fulfilled the requirements for a healthy and clean working atmosphere. Usually the area resided by the child workers were characterised by open drains, garbage dumps and poor sanitation and environment facilities. Ventilation was also not satisfactory. 54% of the households had poor ventilation. Similarly, the majority of house of the working children did not have satisfactory lighting. As many as 54 percent of the workers informed about the poor lighting. Only 46% of the child workers informed that their place had the satisfactory lighting conditions.

These living and working conditions often make home based workers particularly vulnerable to various diseases and had health. In the end it may be worth mentioning that though the Chikan work is available throughout the season, the burden on the workers increases in Summerdays when it becomes quite hot.

SUMMARY

It is evident from the survey that the working conditions were far from satisfactory. The long working hours often left no time for the child workers for any other household activities. These long hours have several detrimental effects on the child worekers. These working conditions cause tremendous damage to the physical health of the child workers and hence they grew into a weak adult in the future.

When a child workere is made to perform dull, laborious and repetitive tasks day in and day out, his mind becomes tired out. At this young age, they should be free from responsibilities but circumstances forced them to become wage earners. Consequently they lose the inclination for formal education.

It is very difficult to regulate the working hours and

conditions of work without the proper implementation of legislation. Since it was not possible to ban the children to work and that too in the unorganised sector, a new legislation should be enacted to regulate conditions of the child workers working in their houses. Besides passing such a legislation the authorities should take other steps to improve the environmental conditions of the localities which are predominantly inhabited by the child workers of Chikan Industry.

ECONOMIC DETERMINANT OF CHILD WORKERS

Wages

Once of the hardest and unfortunate aspect of poverty is that children are required to work as wage earners and India is a country where more than 60% of the population still lives below the poverty line and the parents, who are caught in the web of poverty, put the child to work and marginally increase the family income by their labour. However the family remains as poor as ever.

During the survey we found that every household had 2 to 3 child workers along with the adult females doing the Chikan work. It has also been found that although with the increasing numbers of years of employment, their works become better and better and yet their wages remain the same as before.

Table 33: Showing the piece-work rates

	Rates given per piece of work	
Items	Workdone	Rate (in Rs.)
Kurta-1 plain	Murri	20
Kurta-1 Darajdar	Murr	12
Kurta-3	Murri Phanda	8.25
Kurta-4	Bakhia	7
Kurta tericott/4	Bakhia	5
Saree fine Wayal	Phanda	6

,, ,, ,,	Bakhia	75
Salwar Suit Tericott	Phanda Murri	60
,, ,, ,,	Bakhia	25
Paijama Suit Tericott	Phanda Murri	25
,, ,, ,,	Bakhia	25
Salwar Suit Cotton	Phanda Murri	25
,, ,, ,,	Bakhia	25
Paijama Suit Cotton	Phnada Murri	25
,, ,, ,,	Bakhia	25
Saree Argandi 5-2	Phanda Murri	115
Saree Argandi 5-3	Phanda	75
,, ,,	Bakhia	60
Saree Wayal 5-9	Phanda	45
,, ,,	Bakhia	25
Blouce piece	Phanda	7
,, ,,	Bakhia	5
Dupatta Border Pallu	Border	20
,, Jaldar	Jaal	30

Most of the children now have permanently adopted doing 'Chikan Work'. Most of these workers are not paid daily wages but get payment according to piece rate. This payment depends upon the volume of embroidery done on the piece. Sometimes more than one person works on the piece because not every girl knows all the stitches like phanda, tepchi, murri and so on.

The Table 33 only suggests that hte child workers are not paid according to their hours of work but on piece rate basis. No effort till now has been made to get the authorities to enfroce minimum wages. The child is not paid according to the number of hours that she puts in doing the Chikan embroidery work. The child workers informed that if they were paid more, they would definitely make an effort to improve the quality of their work. Since they were paid the same wage irrespective of the quality of work done, they did not bother about the quality of work.

SUMMARY

The child workers are not paid any fixed wages. They are paid on piece-rate basis. The pathetic situation about the payment system in the Chikan work is that quality of work is not given due importance in payment of wages to the workers. Consequently the payment of wages is also not related to the number of years put in by the child workers. Often group of 2-3 child workers work on a piece and hence the payment on that piece is shared by the workers doing on the said piece and hence the economic condition of the workers does not improve.

LIVING ENVIRONMENT DETERMINANT OF CHILD WORKERS

Housing

Various reports have confirmed that India's urban population is constantly rising over the years. The constant rising in the population has further aggravated the urban housing problem. In most of the large Indian cities we find narrow and congested lanes with improper drainage, lack of drinking water and inadequate housing facilities. The study of housing conditions of the households in which children are found working in the Chikan Industry, is of permanent importance as environment plays a major role in determining the development of the personality of the working child. The impact of these conditions, which are sub-human to a large extent, on the child, is so immense that it leaves a permanent scar on physical as well as moral development of the child's personality. Lack of proper accommodation is harmuful for mental, physical and moral development of the working child as well as the entire family. These houses lack privacy, and this has certain psychological repercussion on the growing members. The small and kutchcha houses offers little or no protection from rain, cold or sweltering heat conditions.

The follwing table throws light on the types of the hoses in relation to their ownership.

Table 34: Shwoing Distribution of Child Workers According to the Type of Dwelling and Ownership

The above Table shows that majority of the houses were pucca as well as owned by the families of the child workers. Only 18 per cent of houses were semi katchcha and 22 per cent on rent. It is also worth mentioning that the amount of rent varied from Rs. 100-300 depending upon the accommodation and the standard of house and the locality.

Type of house	Number of child	%	Own	%	Rented	%
Pucca	41	82	30	77	11	100
Semi-Katchcha	9	18	9	23	--	
Total	50	100	39	100	11	100

The following table contains information regarding the extent of accommodation available in the houses occupaied by the workers.

Table 35: Showing the Distribution of the Child Workers by the Number of Rooms Available in the Worker's House

Number of Rooms	Number of child workers	Percentage
One room only	22	42
1-2 rooms	15	30
More than 2 rooms	13	26
Total	50	100

From the above Table we find that out of the total households surveyed 42 per cent were having one room and 30 per cent houses had 1-2 rooms while only 26 per cent of the houses had more than two rooms. The Table 11.1 had shown that 18% families were living in semi-kutchcha houses. These houses were made of mostly small bricks and thatches whereas in pucca houses the walls were brick-laid cemented.

The essential aspect of the urban housing is whether the houses contained the following facilities-

1. Water facilities,
2. Ventilation,
3. Lighting,
4. Latrine,
5. Kitchen and
6. Water supply.

It was found that most of the families had municipal water connections. These of the had hand-pumps installed in their houses. Seven household were using water from public water taps in the near vicinity. Toilet facilites were available only in some houses. Only 10 houses holds had proper flush fitted toilets. The rest had katchcha toilets.

It was interesting to know that most of the pucca houses had electric connections and some of the kutcha houses had also electricity connections.

All the pucca houses had some clean corners which were used as kitchens, even the kutchcha houses too managed the same corner to use as kitchen.

SUMMARY

To conclude, we can say that the over flowing drains, big heaps of refuse, congested and crowded living quarters, absence of toilets etc. are harmful for the child workers and their family members. The Lucknow Mahapalika should take effective measures to ensure that centain basic civic amenties are available specially in the area which are pre-dominantly occupied by Chikan Workers.

RECREATIONAL DETERMINANT OF CHILD WORKERS

The word 'recreation' means the proper and constructive use of leisure time by the individual. This gives dimension and release of tensions from monotonous long working hours. Therefore recreation is an essential factor for the proper physical, mental and spiritual growth of an individual, specially the working child.

Leisure time is one of the gifts of a mature civilization. The way leisure time is spent determines to a long extent the culture of the individual and collectively of the country as a whole. It has been rightly said that leisure is work's greatest achievement.

During the course of survey, it was found that the children who were found doing Chikan embroidery were all girls. They mostly came from the Muslim families where purdah system is very strictly observed. As soon as girls cross the age of puberty they are not allowed to go out of the house alone.

It is also striking to not that as the wages of the Chikan Workers are fixed on piece-rate basis the work for pretty long hours with little break of time in between the work. Even holidays and Sundays are not spared in working.

By discussing with the child labourers it was found that the girls sometimes wathched televisions, visited movies along with their family members for their recreation.

One of the most obvious avtivities of children is 'play' a spontaneous, free, joyful and pleasurable activity for them. By observing it could be inferred that the child workers could not devote their free time to this natural urge because there was hardly any place for playing games in their homes and neighbourhood.

An important indication that children are imaginative can be seen from the imaginray work they indulge in that is the drawing of the motives.

We have already noted that girls have less free time boys. They are less free than boys to come and go to at will. They must help the household work, which is less required of the boys. The following Table present rank orders of the recreational activities preferred by the child workers.

This Table transpires that the child workers being the females prefer singing and dancing with top most priority, followed by Radio listening, Indoor games, movie-visiting, dramatic displays, outdoor games and hobby activities, which include collection of photographs, coins, painting, sewig and embroidery etc. in that order.

Talbe 36: Shwoing the Rank Order of Recreational Activities prefered by Child Workers

Recreational activities	Rank Order	Frequency N=50
Singing and Dancing	1	23
Radio listening	2	21
Television viewing	3	20
Indoor games	4	19
Movie visiting	5	17
Dramatic display	6	16
Outdoor games	7	8
Hobby activities	8	7

The recreational needs of a person become greater when we see the nature of the work done by him which requires long working hours and concentration in performance of the activities. Therefore steps should be taken by the government to develop some parks and playgrounds in the vicinity of houses occupied by child workers to provide recreational facilities therefor the children. These parks should be built in the very area from which the children come. Recreation is very important for the proper physical and mental growth of the child workers.

SUMMARY

The above discussion makes it clear that female child workers have less time than male child workers. In between the working hours they also have to assist in household activities. Nonetheless, the female child workers have some preferences for the recreational activities. Singing and Dancing,

Radio listening. Television viewing, Indoor games are some of the preferences of the child workers for their recreational activities.

Recommendations and Suggestions

Child Labour in any industry and Chikan Industry in particular, is a grim reality, a reality that has to be accepted for many years to come in the future too. This is because it is not realistically possible nor practical to totally abolish Child Labour in India. Several reasons contribute towards this thinking, The foremost reasons being that most of the children come from families with very low income, though their wages are very nominal yet they supplement the family income. Secondly, these child workers do not have any education or training that could be of use to them while looking for alternate jobs. They earn very little which is in most cases the income of Rs. 10/- to Rs. 100/- per month. Sitting in their homes and being mostly females and observing purdah has made them totally unaware of changes going on out of four walls of their homes. New educational facilities on the lines of the condensed course have to be provided more and more to meet the needs of these children. If these children are forced to attend conventional schools, then they will join the teeming millions of education unemployed youth which will increase their frustration and aggravate their pitiable conditions.

When the parents were informally asked why Mahajans preferred employment of children in Chikan Industry, several reasons were advanced. Some of them were as follows:

If the child started work at an early age, the quality of work is bound to improve and on maturity they attain the height of good work in Chikan. In turn these children supplement the meagre family imcome.

The real reason for employing children is stated to be the economic one. The payment of low wages leads to Mahajan's higher profit. The mahajans convince the working children by saying that they were doing a favour to the children's families.

The reasons given above cannot be used as justification for the perpetuation of child labour in the Chikan Industry. As was pointed out earlier, early employment fo the child retards his physical and mental development and leads to reduction in his or her earning capacity in the future years.

The recommendations for improving the conditions of children employed in the Chikan Industry can be summarized as under:

1. Inclusion of children doing chikan work in Child Labour (Protection and Regulation) Act 1986.

2. All the schemes under Child Welfare Services being run by Government be so directed so as to reach the children employed in Chiakn Industry, their families and communities. Proper monitoring should be undertaken by Government officials to ensure that they are being run properly.

3. Meeting the vasic needs of the children employed in the Chikan Industry viz, health, nutrition and recreation.

4. Undertaking measures to meet the basic needs of the families to which these children belong.

5. Undertake long term measures in order to regulate the working conditions of children in Chikan Industry.

6. In August 1987, the National Child Labour Policy was adopted comprising three thrust areas, namely, is legal action plan; (ii) Focasing of General Welfare and development programme on child labour and the families. (iii) A project based 'Plan of Action'. The policy will works out strategy for strict and effective inforcement of the child labour Act, 1980 and utilize the on going development programme for the benefit of working children and their families.

7. Jawahar Rojgar Yojna (JRY) launch by the Govt. in 1989 aims at providing relief to the weaker section of society. If the benefit of JRY do percolate down to the real target beneficiaries, the picture of child labour that would emerged is the

1991 census would probably be quiet different, and there might actually be a downward trend.

The suggestions listed above need further clarification. These are as under:

I. Inclusion of children doing chikan work in the Child Labour (Protection and Prohibition) Act 1986:

The child labour (protection and prohibition) Act 1986 was passed in 1986 with the main objective:

"To ban the employment of children in certain specified occupations" and to "regulate conditions of work of children in employment where they are not prohibited from working."

The schedule which lists the occupation in which children are prohibited from working does not include chikan work. The provision relating to working consitions also can not be applied since chikan is a home-based industry.

The first step should be to include Chikan embroidery and other home-based work in the unorganised sector under the purview of the Child Labour (Protection and Prohibition) Act 1986 with the help of a suitable amendment. This law was passed mainly to regulate working conditions and in some cases prohibits employment of children mainly in the unorganised sector has ignored a large number of occupations in which children are employed. The earlier discussion in the main body of the report pointed out that working conditions are far from satisfactory and because of the unorganised nature of the Chikan Industry, nothing has been achieved through the Child Labour (Prohibition and Regulation) Act 1986. Thus, the first and foremost need is to regulate working conditions of child workers engaged in the Chikan Industry through the following steps:

(1) These children should be so organised that they sit in a room which might be in their home or in their neighbourhood with proper facilities like lighting, ventilation, safety of build-

ing and so on. The supervisor, in charge of these workshops should be a local muslim woman whom the parents can trust and who will ensure that no exploiting incidence takes place.

(2) Steps should also be taken to ensure that a child does not work for more than a certain period of time as laid down by the Law. The child should be entitled to a rest interval of atleast one hour.

(3) The entire work period including the rest interval shall not exceed six hours.

(4) Inspectors from the local Labour Office should came for regular inspection of these workshops to ascertain facts such as:

(a) Address of workshop to which communications regarding the workshop should be sent.

(b) Name and location of the workshop.

(c) The nature of the occupation carried on in the workshop.

(5) All these workshop so establised shall be asked to maintain a register of children employed or permitted to work in any establishment. The register shall contain:

(a) The names and data of birth of every child employed or permitted to work.

(b) The work and duration of work of every child and also the rest he is entitled to.

(c) The nature of work whether he is doing embroidery stitching or any other work in Chikan work.

(6) Regular inspection should be made of these work centres with a view to checking the following :

(a) Cleanliness of the place of work.

(b) Proper ventilation.

(c) Adequate lighting,

(d) Provision of drinking water.

(e) Provision of toilets.

(f) Maintenance and safety.

(7) For above mantioned purpose, the Government should appoint inspectors.

(8) The Supervisors and their employer shall be punished in accordance with the Law, if necessary.

(9) The Government should take steps to see that the training centres being run by those who have won awards offered by the U.P. Government and the Central Government for excellence in handicrafts are being properly organised. These people are given Government grants to run training centres for girls who do not know any Chikan work. But in practice these people take the girls who already know Chikan work. They get orders from the shops, and make these girls do their work and pay them very low wages and keep the profit for themselves. This looses the basic objective of the programme. Even the stipend that these girls are supposed to be given is pocketed by the person in charge.

Proper selection should be done to ensure that these girls selected for the work actually do not know any Chikan work and that they belong to the family of chikan workers. The course whould be for a period of one year. After the completion of the course, a final examinantion should be held and accordingly grade certificate should be given. These certificates should be used by the girls when they apply for jobs such as Quality Inspector in some Government agency.

II. Implementation of Child Welfare Scheme being run by the Government

Although there are various Child Welfare Schemes being run by the Government, they have not reached the children in the Chikan Industry. So steps should be taken to ensure that these programmes reach the children in Chikan Industry. Some of the programmes that the Government is running are:

1. Integrated Child Development Scheme (ICDS).

2. Supplementary Nutrition Programme (SNP).

3. Maternity and Child Health Centres (MCH).

4. Provision of free education at the primary level.

5. Mid-day meals.

6. Scholarship for higher education.

7. Creches and day care centres.

8. Grants to voluntary organisations for providing recreational facilities.

III. Meeting the Basic needs of the Children in the Chikan

Each basic of the child, i.e., health, food nutrition, education and recreation, has to be recognized in its own right and while planning programmes all of them have to be integrated as they are all inter dependent in nature.

The basic needs of the children employed in the Chikan Industry are common to all children but there are some additional needs arising out of the problems that are unique to this Industry.

The basic needs determinates of the children are:

(A) Health

The overall health situation of the children is quite depressing. The following recommendations can be made, keeping the health needs of children into consideration:

(i) Regular health check-up by a Pedratrician and provision of treatment, if necessary.

(ii) Immunization programmes.

(iii) Regular testing of eyes with provision of corrective measures when necessary.

(iv) Imparting health education to children with special em phasis on aspects concerning the Chikan work including teaching the correct postures for sitting while at work.

(v) Provision of mobile clinics by voluntary organisations.

(vi) Proper and regular disposal of garbage in the areas occupied by the child workers should be done by the Lucknow Nagar Mahapalika as garbage dumps increase the risk of epidemics if not done regularly.

(vii) The drains which had not been cleaned may bacomes a breeding ground for all kinds of germs. Drains in these areas should be cleaned regularly by the Lucknow Nagar Mahapalika.

(viii) Congested and bad housing increases the susceptibility to various kinds of diseases and is harmful from the health, hygiens and safety point of views, Tuberculosis is rampart in these areas primarily because of poor housing conditions, kutchacha houses provide little protection from rains, bitter cold or scorching heat. Therefore steps should be taken to improve the living conditions of these areas inhabited by child workers engaged in the Chikan Industry.

(ix) Since most of the people surveyed were reluctant to go to the Government Hospitals for treatment because of reasons such as heavy rush and long queues, expensive medicines; so Government doctors should make regular visits to these areas and check-up the children and their families regularly.

(B) Nutrition

The most important need of the child is adequate food. There is little purpose in planning to safeguard measures and protect him from disease and accidents if he is likely to succumb to malnutrition.

The nutrition status, as previously stated is far from satisfactory. The recommendation with regard to the food and nutritional requirements of the children engaged in Chikan are:

(i) Providing supplementary nutrition with special emphasis on the need for a balance diet.

(ii) Imparting nutritional education to mothers and children.

(C) Education

Education is of particular relevance in under-developed countries where it is an indispensable instrument for economic and social development:

At any given time, around half or more children of the primary school going age may be out of school. This keeps the goal of universal primary education rather distant. The majority of the non-school going children including girls are burdened with household courses or earning a living for adding to the income of the family."

The following recommendations specify how the current educational programme can be modified and adopted to suit the needs of the children doing Chikan work.

(i) Since these girls work for an average of six to seven hours and also do household work, it is not possible for them to attend formal school. Classes should be held either in the mornings or after they complete their work. The duration of the classes should not exceed two hours a day.

(ii) Due to the heavy work load, classes should be held on alternate days.

(iii) Education should enable them to do the basic mathematics, reading and writing.

(iv) Apart from 'conventional' type of education the other methods of imparting education and practicals, use of mass-media, institutional visits, should be used.

To reach the first goal of the universal education it is necessary to convince the planners and administrators that education embraces much more than 'academic' skills and has to have a curriculum both explicit and implicit which can build skills useful for household, for occupational purpose, for problem solving and for continuous self-learning in the field of work.

Thus schemes should be started for providing functional education with adult education. The course should be the one set by the NCERT, New Delhi. There year courses should be started. During the courses they should be given education and also they should be made to make samples so that the quality of their work improves.

(v) These girls should be taught how to organize themselves by social workers and voluntary organizations, already working in this field.

The girls should be awareness classes about their rights and status by Labour Inspectors and other social workers.

The girls can then organize themselves into cooperatives with a minimum membership of twenty. The girls themselves should look after the marketing of the finished products.

The U.P. Government should give loans of Rs. 25,000/- for self employment which these girls can utilize. These cooperatives should be used for the upliftment of the families living there and also the entire community.

It is only when they are educated and made economically independent, will the mahajans stop exploiting them. It is because they are uneducated and unorganized that they are being exploited by the mahajans. These cooperatives can later on be merged into a trade union which will fight for their rights.

(vi) Steps should be taken to improve the standard of education for these child workers. Since these children come from Muslim families, importance should be given for teaching Urdu, which should be included in the school curriculum.

(vii) Schools should be opened exclusively for girls in Daliganj as also for child workers living in other localities. The Company on Child Labour states:

"The education curriculum for each area should be drawn up keeping in view the basic requirements of the invironment. The present craze for uniformity in the educational policy needs to be noted down. At present there are not satisfactory provisions for providing educational facilities for child workers under Labour Laws."

(D) Recreation

Recreation is important for the physical, mental and spiritual growth of the child. The following recreational activities are recommended for the children doing Chikan Work:

(i) Since children sit for such long stretches which affect their physical growth, steps should be taken to promote physical exercise.

(ii) Since mental and creative abilities of the child are limited, appropriate forms of recreation for improving the child's creative and mental abilities are greatly needed.

(iii) Since they have little scope for developing their general awareness, so their interests, hobbies, etc. should be organized at their place itself to give them greater exposure.

The Reoprt of the Committee on Child Labour states:

"If facilities for recreation or cultural activities are provided either at the place of work or residence, children will be able to regenerate themselves after a day of monotonous toil. Otherwise it will increase juvenile delinquency.

IV. Meeting the needs of the Child Worker's Family and Community

An important aspect of child workers includes the family in any programme of services being organized for them. The family is an integral part of the child's life. The services which benefit the family shall also benefit the child.

The recommendations pertaining to the family and the community are as follows:

1. Adult education classes should be organised for the parents with a focus for bringing an awareness in them regarding the legal provisions available in the Chikan work.

2. Education on health, nutrition and child rearing should be given to the mothers of these children.

3. Education the women will broaden their horizons thereby bringing about a change in their attitude which is important to the child also.

(E) Long Term Measures

The complete eradication of child labour should be a cherished dream in any developing country, though it is difficult to be accomplished. Thus, certain long term measures with a view to arresting the child labour phenomenon should be taken. The following are some long term measures that can be taken while dealing with the problem of Child Labour.

1. Steps should be taken to eradicate poverty as poverty is the root cause of all social evils, especially the child labour. Statistics show that even after four decades of planning, the percentage of population living below the poverty line has infact increased. The programmes being run by the government should reach the beneficiaries, specially families of Chikan workers, thereby increasing their income and reducing the necessity to send their child for work to supplement the family income.

2. Today a growing majority of the child population falls in contex of deprivation, which is born not necessarily so much from economic poverty-but to appropriate technoligies to infrastuctrure and managerial ability, This sort of poverty can not be successfully overcome by improved GNP and per income measures or by enhanced resources but requires deliberate measures to expand the availibility, efficiency as well as the utilization of services and to make them more responsive

to children and their developing needs.

3. The profit margin of the shopkeepers and the mahajans is quite large in the Chikan Industry and hence the worker is exploited.

A system of minimum wages for workers as well as those doing embroidery work should be imposed and implemented effectively. Although prices of product increase, the wages remain the same. Therefore steps should be taken to reduce exploitation.

4. Girls from the cooperatives should be assisted by the U.P. Handicrafts Board to market their goods. The profits should go to the girls themselves.

5. Family planning should be given wide publicity. The large size of families in the lower income group compels them to send their child out to work to supplement the family income. So the norm of small family size should be popularised.

6. Public conciousness and awarness of the ill effects of child labour should be publicized through the mass-media. The public is yet to be awakened to the shocking implications of child labour for the development of the nation.

A wind of change must blow through society and through the minds men, for it is only if men adopt a redical new outlook that the ultimate aim, the elimination of child labour can be achieved.

SUGGESTIONS

The evil of child labour exists in this country mainly because of wide-spread poverty and ignorance; and till these twin problems continue to exist, it will not be possible to affectively tackle the problem of child labour. Since with the present state of development in the country it is impossible to eradicate poverty and ignorance in foreseeable future, it is hardly of any use to talk about abolition of child labour which is not only unrealistic but is also likely to do more harm than good to the million of poverty stricken people in the country who are forced by their awfully poor economic condition to seek the help of their children to come out and work for their existence. Chikan work in some of localities of this city is still the most predominant occupation engaging an overwhelming majority of the families residing there. People depending upon chikan work as their economic pursuit live below the poverty line and hence any step in the form of an attempt to ban child labour in Chikan work will, instead of mitigating and alleviating, will aggravate their sufferings and miseries. What seems to be realistice at the present stage of development is to develop such conditions in which children, instead of being forced to take up employment, may be able to go to school and pursue their studies effectively, and those children, who have unfortunately been driven to work, may also be able to start getting their education and to work in a healthy and congenial atmosphere in such a manner that their involvement in work should not effect development suggestions are being extended which may be taken note of while considering the problem of Child Labour by all those who are interested in it:

1. All out efforts should be made to attack the problem of poverty from all sides by sincerely implementing all developmental programmes directly as well as indirectly concerned with promoting the interests of weaker sections in general and child labour in particular.

2. Since many parents/guardians involve their children in work because they do not understand and realise the significance of education, it is necessary to develop education consciousness among them by making use of all possible means, especially by organi ing adult education programme. The present situation in which educated youngman fail to get suitable employment consonant with their educational attainments and also find it difficult to take up traditional family occupations creates a feeling of uselessness of education in the minds of parents/guardians which in turn gives rise to a feeling of apathy, and in many cases even aversion, towards education. Such

a situation can be retrieved by suitably reorienting the education to meet the demands of reality and by giving it required vocational and technical bias.

3. The constitutional obligation of providing free and compulsory education to all children upto the age of fourteen years should be fulfilled without any further delay. It will be necessary to take the following steps for the fulfilment of this obligation:

(i) Education should be made legally compulsory.

(ii) A chain of educational institutions, within easy reach of children should be established so that any child desirous of getting education may not have to go more than one kilometer.

(iii) Education to children upto 14 years of age should be given free. The present restrtction in U.P. of providing free education to boys up to VI class only should be removed. The facility of free education, without fixing any class limit should be extended to all boys and girls at least up to 14 years.

(iv) The entire expenditure on education of children should be borne by the government.

(v) The school security programme of aid to families with dependent children to suitably compensate parents/guardians for the loss they suffer because of withdrawal of their children from work should be started.

(vi) Community creches should be established in areas having concentration of child workers in order to enable the child looking after the youngones in their families to attend the school.

(viii) For the time being, keeping in view the necessity of children's work in Chikan work, school timings should be suitably adjusted to meet the requirements of Chikan work so that child workers may be able to learn while they earn; and if necessary, formal/non-formal education centres should be started in night with the help of existing voluntary organizations. In case of child workers who have never been or left going to school, the Government should make it obligatory for their employers to provide educational facilities to them.

4. Since some of the child workers hae been destitutes Union Department of Social Welfare has been running a scheme of assistance to voluntary organisations through State Governments/Union territory Administrations for extending both institutional and non-institutional services to children upto 12 years of age, in need of care and protection. There is need for giving preference to volutary organisations coming forward to take up this scheme in rural areas.

5. Since for the time being child labour is a necessary evil, special employment bureau should be set up, to help the needy children in getting such work which neither comes in the way of their schooling nor exerts any serious kind of adverse effect on their personality development. Provisions regarding payment of munimum wages, maintenance of registers and records etc. made under the minimum wages Act should be strictly enforced by strengthening and suitably orienting the implementation machinery and assisting it by developing a cadre of voluntary workers. Provisions regarding penalty for payment of less than the prescrebed minimum rates of wages or less than the amount due to an employee under the Act should be amended on the lines suggested earlier in the context of adult workers; and the general provision of fine of upto Rs. 500/- in case of contravention of any provision of the Act or of any rule or any order made thereunder, should be amended by converting it into an imprisonment upto one year or fine upto Rs. 1000/-.

6. In order to provide opportunity to working girls for supplementing the income of their families by contributing their share to the family fund, it is desirable to develop cooperative societies of these young working girls having responsibility for organising training, making raw material available and selling the produced goods.

7. In order to prepare children for future, it becomes necessary to equip them with certain skills suited to their aptitude. It will, therefore, be desirable to develop suitable aptitude tests keeping in view the Indian conditions and to administer them on both the types of working children viz. those who combine their work with studies and those who are completely involved in work. After ascertaining their aptitude, suitable training shuld be imparted by the Training Institutes/Centres for the child workers in general and in vocations for those working children who combine their work with studies.

8. The Government should immediately enact a comprehensive legislation for Chikan Industry to provide for working hours, rest intervals, overtime, leave and holidays, health, safety and other related welfare.

9. The Government of Uttar Pradesh should effectively enforce the Children Act.

10. As a matter of long-term strategy, a National Children's Code incorporating provisions of the Children Act with model rules and uniform standards and norms regulating employment of children in different occupations should be made. The Code should lay down the minimum age of more than 14 years for entry of children into any employment. The Code should be flexible enough to provide an opportunity to concerned administrative authorities for evolving necessary regulatory means and welfare measures and should prescribe working hours, conditions of work etc.

11. The Government should intiate a dialogue with trade unions at its earliest in order to prepare institutional framework necessary for collective bargaining with regard to improvement in working conditions and conditions of work and to control the magnitude of child labour, specially engaged in the Chikan work.

12. Minimum need programme with all its components should be effectively implemented.

13. Young persons, clubs, libraries and reading rooms fully

equipped with necessary material suited to the taste of the local children should be established by voluntary social welfare agencies which should be given grant-in-aid by the Central Social Welfare Board.

14. The National Children's Board/State Children's Board should more closely associate themselves with problems of Child Labour and should take necessary steps immediately to improve the lot of child workers by checking their exploitation and improving their working conditions and conditions of work.

15. Studies on Child Labour in Chikan Work on bigger scale in different parts of Lucknow city should be sponsored in order to throw light on regional variations in different aspects of Child Labour. This may be helpful in evolving a comprehensive pieces of legislation having uniformity in standards and norms regulating the problem of Child Labour but at the same time making necessary provision for ensuring flexbility to suit regional variations.

16. Seminars, Symposia, Discussions, etc. on various aspects of Child Labour should be organised from time to time, and the problem of Child Labour should be widely publicised through different types of mass-media in order to create awareness of this social evil among people and to motivate them to come forward to gradually eliminate it.

Socio-Economic Determinants of Child Labour in Chikan Industry

One of the major social problems confronting the Government today is that of "Child Labour". Children in the pre-industrial agricultural society worked as helpers in hereditarily determined occupations under the supervision of adult family members. But with the advent of the industrial revolution, the social scenario changed radically. The cild had to work as individual person either under an employer or independently. The enviornment in which he worked endangered his physical health and mental growth and led to his empolitation. The protection and welfare of these children became in issue of social significance. The emergence of welfare consicousness in the world scale has led to the enunciating of several of the welfare measures to meet the problem of child labour, and it has a universal appeal to human conscience.

child labour in a restricted sense, according to V.V. Giri, is: ".....the employment of children in gainpur occupations which are dangerous to their health and denythem the opportunity of development".

As per the 1981 census the total Indian population is 680 million, out of which 264 million or 38.8% of the total population is in the age group 0-14 years. As per the 1981 census the number of working children stands at 13.8 million which constituted 7% of the total labour force according to an ILO study. The national sample survey conducted in 1983 puts the total number of working children at 17.5 million out of which 10.33 million or 59% boys and 7.18 million or 41% are girls.

Lucknow, being the former capital of the province of Oudh, was a centre of fine arts, music and culture. On account of this fact it attracted master craftsmen from the country-over. Although little remains of its past splender and glory, these crafts still continue to flourish in the parts of the old city. These crafts include Mukesh, Chikankari, Zardozi, Gota, Chandi ka waraq, and many others. All these crafts employ thousands of men, women and children and these crafts come under the purview of the unorganised sector.

In the Chikan Industry, as in all other crafts industries, there are a large number of children working, Chikan might be described as fine embroidery done with different coloured threads on various clothing items. Different types of stitches may be used depending upon the type of pattern to be embroidered. Some times white threads are also used for the embroidery.

Causes of Child Labour

The causes of child labour vary from place to place and

are numerous. But the general causes of Child Labour are:

1. Poverty

Poverty is the root cause of all social evils and this is to exception. It was found that the living wage of an adult worker is closely related to child labour.

During the survey it was found that 62% of the households came from very low income groups that is Rs.0-800 per month.

2. Increased Profits

Child labour is one of the cheapest commodities. It was found that children in the Chikan Industry did a better work than the adults and were also paid less. Children are exploited economically and it is more kkprofitable to employ children than adults.

3. Easily available commodity

Children compared to adults are more easily available.

4. Lack of Educational Facilities

Lack of educational facilities in the areas surveyed is one of the major causes of child labour. Private schools are expensive and every one can not afford them.

5. Illiteracy and Ignorance of Parents

The survey revealed that 44% of fahters and 100% of mothers were completly illiterate. Only 6% of the faters and received formal education.

6. Tradition

It was found that in the majority of the households surveyed,chikan was family occupation.

7. Unorganised nature of Child Labour

The unorganised nature of child labour has led to their increasing exploitation since they are not able to organise themselves into trade unions to fight for their rights.

Education

It is through education that society imparts its skills and knowledge to the next generation. It is said that the child of today is the leader of tomorrow. Education has been defined as the "Art of developing and cultivating physical, intellectual, aesthetic and moral faculties of the individual with a view to enabling him to respond positively to demands and responsibilities of his social being. In all developing countries including India, there is neither lack of awareness of the importance of education, primary, secondary, intermediate and higher nor any shortage of commitment to achieving to educated society. In spiteof provision for free and compulsory education upto the age of 14 years in Part IV of the Indian Constitution, the 1981 census reveals that 64% of the population can neither read or write. The directive principals of State Policy of the Indian Constitution (Article 45).

"The State shall endeavour to provide within ten years of the commencement of the constitution free and compulsory education for all children upto the age of 14 years".

Although the Indian Constitution has been in existence for more than 4 decades, yeat the percentage of literacy in the country has not gone above 35 per cent.

In this survey, we found that only 5 children or 10% were currently attending school. 19 children or 38% has dropped out of school while 26 children or 52% had never been to school.

This clearly shows that although the government is giving due importance to education by including it in the Five Years Plans, a lot still needs to be done in this field.

Health

The National Policy or Health reiterates the commitment of the goal of health for all by the year 2000 A.D.

Article 47 of Directive Principles of State Policy reveals that the State shall strive to raise the nutritional standards of the children.

Despite all these statements the infant mortality rate is 125/1000.

The child is particularly vulnerable to certain health hazards because of the nature of her work. Majority of the children surveyed had eye problems. Some complained of bakaches and other armaches, while some also complained of fiddiness and headaches. 45 or 90% children had not been innoculated. Only 6 or 12% children had received treatment.

It can be said that general public is quite indifferent and apathetic towards immunisation. The main cause of this apathy is the lack of awareness and information regarding the benefits of immunization on people's part.

Nutrition

Nutrition is the world's major causing more deaths than famine, yet lacking the drama and excitement of a crisis. Malnutrition makes the children vulnerable to diseases. The Foundation of India reported that out of 23 million children born every year only 3 million are physically fit, productive and intellectually capable.

Only 20 children or 40% could be catergorized as healthy. 30 or 60% of them suffered from malnutrition.The health of the majority of the child workers had been very poor.

Recreation

Recreation is essential for the physical,mental and spiritual growth of the child. It is process of socializing. The long working hours and monotonous type of work that the children to leaves them little or no time to recreate themselves. This impedes the development of their creative and imaginative abilities.

Working Conditions

The condition of working children is far from satisfactory. Article 24 of the Indian Constitution relating to fundamental rights states that "No child below the age of 14 years shall be employed in any factory or mine or engaged in any other hazardous employment.

Since it is neither feasible nore realistically possible to obtain child labour under present conditions, Child Labour (Prohibition and Regulation) Act 1986 was passed to regulated the working condition of these children. But unfortunately Chikan being a home-based industry and that too unorganized in nature, this legislation can not be applied.

It was found that 64% of the children worked for more than 6 hours a day. Some are even working for upto 8 hours a day. For a child of less than 14 years this was overburdening.

It was found that a large percentage of the children started work at a very young age and hence had been working for more than 5 years.

It has been also been observed that if a girls was employed for more than 5 years,her working hours decrease, this is because of the fact that as they grow older they have to help more in household courses and also look after the younger siblings of the house.

Most of the children that is 34 or 68% of them worked at home. Another 16 or 32% worked at the neighbours.

The condition under which the children worked was inhuman. These children all worked at home or in the neighbourhood in rooms which had no proper ventilation. Most of the houses were not even clean.

Besides passing such a legislation the authorities should take other steps to improve the invironmental conditions of the localities which are perdominantly inhabited by the child workers of Chikan Industry.

Wages

More than 60% of Indian population lives below the

subsistence level. It is because of this that the full economic value of the child is not recognised and she is paid much less than what the adults get. It is the economic necessity that forces parents to send their child out to work instead of educating them. It is cheaper to employ the child than to employ the adult.

The Constitutional provisions as stated in Article 39 of the Directive Principles of State Policy that "The State shall make provisions to ensure that the under age of children is not exploitedand that citizens are not forced out of economic necessity to enter into vocations unsuited to their age and strength". It further goes on to state that "Children and youth are protected against exploitation and natural and moral abandonment".

During the survey, the reason the children gave for entering this vocation was poverty, family trade and the fact that it required no special training.

The child workers were not paid any fixed wages. They were paid on piece-rate basis. The pathetic situation about the payment system in the Chikan work is that quality of work is not given due consideration in payment of wages is also not related to the number of years put in by the child workers. Often group of 2-3 child workder work on a piece and hence the payment on that peice is shared by the workers doing on the said piece and hence the economic conditions of the workers does not improve.

There was no concept of overtime. The children were given orders and it was upto them to complete it in a day or a week. They would be paid accordingly.

Housing and Civic Amenities

The environmental conditions of the child workers are characterized by garbage dumps, overflowing drains, absence of toilets, congested and damp living conditions and so on. All theseact as an impendiment in the proper physical and mental development of the child. Majority of the families lived in single roomed houses, while some were found living in kutcha houses. Barring a few of the families, all the others fetchedwater from the community taps. No facility of toilets existed in their houses and they used as the nearby fields as toilets.

The Lucknow Mahapalika should take effective measures to ensure that certain basic civic amenities are available specially in the areas which are pre-dominantly occupied by child workers.

Family Background

Since the family plays a very important role in the development of the child, a study of the family background of the child was also undertaken.

Most of the families surveyed were large families.

Determining family income is important since the major cause of child labour is poverty. 31 families or 62% had family income less than Rs.800 a month, while another 19 families or 38% earned above Rs.800 a month.

Since most of the parents were uneducated, their occupations were also those that required no educational background. Their occupations were primarily those in the unorganized sector such a rickshaw puller, vegetable vendors, hawkers, labourers, factory workers and government servants.

Ignorance and illiteracy of the parents are the causes of child labour. 90% of their mothers were illiterate and 70% of the children's fathere were completely illiterate.

The fact that women observe purdah makes them psychologically dependen, backward and socially unaware. This makes them totally limited in their outlook. It was foundthat in many of the families Chikan work was a family tradition.

RECOMMENDATIONS

The recommendations for improving the conditions of

children in the Chikan Industry are as follows:

1. Inclusion of Chikan Work on home-based work in the Child Labour (Prohibition and Regulation) Act 1986. Ensure that the Government Programme being run for children reach the beneficiaries, their families and their communities.

2. Meet the basic need such as health, duration and nutrition al, educaional and recreational needs of the children.

3. Steps should be taken to ensure that the standards and conditions of the family as well as the community background plays an important role in determining the future personality of the child.

4. Undertaking long term measures with the ultimate aim of improving the conditions of the children with the hope of abolishing child labour althogether. This can be done by implementing income, generating programme, self employment programmes so that the income of the families whose children are engaged in Chikan Industry so that they are not forced out of economic necessity to send their children out of work. Minimum wages for home-based workers specially those doing embroidery should be introduced and steps should be taken to set up a cooperative union of these girls. They should be run by these girls with the girls themselves doing marketing, embroidery increasing the publicity of the need for small families so that they are not forced out of economic necessity to send their children out to work. Also publicity about the evils of child labour should be taken up on a large scale.

Children are the seedlings of human resource development and deserve principal attentionas the inputs of present genera tion for the future development of India. If this is not done, then the world risks a great loss both personal and global. "Children of today are the citizens of tomorrow".

Child Labour in Brass Industry

The Government of India has been greatly concerned about the plight of child labour in varous sectors of employment in the country. Inspite of the fact that employment of children is banned under various Acts, socio-economic comoulsions force children to work. The result is that their education, health, physical and mental development are nglected and they have hardly any future except drudery and exploitation. What is worse, is that their working conditions are most unsatisfactory, the working hours are too long, the wages paid are low and often they do not get a weekly day off.

It is clear in such a situation, where children are forced do work due to proverty, mere enforcement of the legal orovisions banning child labour will be counter-productive and only add to the misery of the poor families from which the child workers come. Child labour has been the focus of several Government committee and of numerous studies carried out under the auspices of the Ministery of Labour. The Government of India established in 1981 a Central Advisory Board on Child Labour, headed by the Union Labour Minister, to review the implementation of existing legislation and welfare measures for working children, review the progress of such measures and identify industries and areas where there must be a progressive elimination of child labour. In December 1986, the government passed the Child Labour (Prohibition and Regulation) Act to prohibit the empioyment of children in certain hazardous occupations and processes and to regulate the employment of children in non-prohibited employments. The Act also provides for setting up of a Technical Advisory Committee to advise the Government on the additional industries and sectors which are hazardous to children and in which the employment of children below 14 years should be banned so that a gradual reduction and elimination of child labour can be achived. The Act was followed by a National Policy on Child Labour which of child labour and outlines the action to be taken to benefit and improve the lot of the child workers.

The conclusions that emerge from the various studies on child labour and a review of the experience of government so far are that, notwithstanding the large number of legislations enacted to provide legal protection to children working in factories, mines, plantionas, shops and commercial establishments, etc. and to regulate their these legislations has not been effective and that the provisions, for health and educational development are grossly inadequate. The possibilities for the application of the full force of legislation in unorganised sectors where pronounced are also severely limited. Even if it were possible, it may not necessarily be in the best interest of economic situation of the families concerned. Child labour, however, objectionable it may be, will continue to persist so long as low incomes, high ratios and limited resources are required to contribute, even if modestly to meagre family income.

The problem of child has two distinct but related dimensions: a quantitative aspect, i.e., the quantum and incidence of child labour, and a qualitative aspect, namely the conditions of work and terms of employment. These two aspects must, however, be viewed jointly. A high and growing incidence of child labour other things equal; leads to greater adult unemployment and under-employment, lower child wage rates and greater child exploitation, such as excessive and uninterrupted hours of work, physical and psychological abuse, towards all of which children are far more vulnerable than other groups of workes of. Conversely, a reduction in the incidence of child labour can lead to increased adult earnings and improvements in overall employment and working condition and thus support efforts at improving, promoting and protecting the welfare of children. Therefore, public policy in the field of child labour must encampass these dimensions and aim at:

first, the prohibition of child labour in work which is hazardous to their health and well being.

second, the improvement of the conditions under which children work (where such work is non-hazardous and not banned by law) protection of such children from exploitation, and access to emproved nutrition and minimum levels of educaiton, health protection and skill development.

third, the gradual abolition of child labour by adopting measures that bear on the factors that generate and sustain it.

With this in mind, this pilot project has been formulated. This project is intended to cover children employed in the brassware industry in Moradabad, Uttar Pradesh. Although these constitute the primary target population, the beneficiaries would also include: (a) the parents of these children, and (b) low income and disadvantaged groups who will have benefited directly or and icome-generating schemes and social services.

Objectives

*Long-term Objectives:*The ultimate objectives are:

(a) the elimination of child labour, and

(b) the physical and mental development of children and their protection against exploitation.

Immediate Objectives: The Immediate objectives are:

(a) improvement in health, nutritional status, working conditions, literacy and skill level of the child workers included in this project, and

(b) reduction in the incidence of child labour in the project area.

Background and Context

The brass-ware industry of Moradabad is a traditional industry of Uttar Pradesh. There are factories and more than 7,000 workshops in which various processes are carried on. The important places where the brassware industry is localised at Moradabsad are: Barvlan, Lalbagh, Lal Masjid, Faizgnj, Niyaria Mohalla, Peorjady, Duluya Bagh, Kachcha Bagh, Divan Bagh, etc.

The National Industry Development Corporation, New Delhi carried out a study of metal handicrafts during 1981. The survey identified various processes in the brassware industry at Moradabad. Table 1 indicates the number of units and the total employmetn in these units as ascertained during the survey. The units are all small scale. The registered factories where the more sophisticated work and diminishing work is undertaken have not many of these children were below 14 years of age.

The Uttar Pradesh Labour Department also carried out a sample survey during August 1986 and found out that children below the age of 14 years were employed in foundries, engraving and polishing units. All these jobs are taken up at workshops mostly situated at the dweling places of the craftsmen. Usually children belonging to the families of the craftsman assist their parents in these workshops, but roughly 25% of the children engaged in these jobs are employees drawn from other houses. Roughly 3600 children are deployed in 1800 foundries, 1400 children are engaged in 700 units of engraving and 2400 children are employed in 1200 polishing units, 25% of this strength of 7400 comes to 1850. Thus the children who are required to be rehabilitated, have been estimated to be normally in the range of 1800 to 2000.

Table 1: Break-up of Units of Brassware Industry at Moradabad

Nature of job	Total No. of units	Men	Women	Children	Total
	2	3	4	5	6
Shaping	425	1860	23	296	2179
Polishing	1190	4060	284	1387	5739
Welding	431	746	--	18	764
Casting	2150	6072	276	1872	8220
Enamelling	85	712	63	96	871
Scrapping	890	4346	386	2193	6925
Electoplating	256	1853	212	1613	3678
Engraving	1560	721	--	91	812
Total	6987	20378	1244	7566	29188

Content and Objectives

i) Reduce and ultimately eliminate through strict enforcement of the Factories Act, 1948, the U.P. State Shops and Establishments Act, 1962 and the Child Labour (Prohibition and Regulation) Act, 1986, the employment of children below 14 years in the industry.

ii) Raise the income levels of the families of the child workers by covering them under existing income generating schemes such as IRDP, NREP, RLEGP, etc. and other income-generating schemes of the State Government or the Central Government in the area.

(iii) Provide non-formal education to the child workers and to their parents.

(iv) Provide better health care to the child workers.

(v) Improve the conditions of work and the terms of employment in the industry.

(vi) Improve the nutritional levels of the child workers.

(vii) Raise the general awareness and social consciousness of people of the area.

Enforcement of Child Labour Laws

Employment of children below 14 years is prohibited in factories under the Factories Act, 1948 and employment of children below 12 years is prohibited in smaller workshops under the U.P. State Shops and Commerciai Establishments Act. Unfortunately, the employment of children in the brassware industry in both factory and non-factory establishments has been continuing for years inspite of these provisions. To ensure that no child below 14/12 years is employed in the industry, it is necessary to have both the Factories Act, 1948 and the U.P. State Shops and Establishments Act, 1962, strictly implemented. It will also be necessary to enfoce the Minimum Wages Act and other Acts to ensure that children between 12 years and 14 years employed in shops and establishments are protected.

With the commencement of this project, the Inspectorate under the Labour Department, U.P. posted in the Moradabad Region will give due priority to the enforcement of the labour laws relating to child workers. Every Labour Inspector will be required to carry out at least 10 inspections every month. The total yearly target of inspections per Inspector will be 12-15 units. The target of prosecutions will be 100% of the major breaches detected but not removed after inspection. Similarly in case where children between 12 years and 14 years employed in establishments and workshops engaged in the brassware industry are paid les than the prescribed minimum rates of wages, claim cases will have to be filed in all cases of breaches which have not been removed after inspection.

The inspections requires to be carried out as also prosecutions and claim cases required to be filed will be rigorously monitored by the Regional Labour Commissioner, Moradabad, so that an impact is created in the minds of the employers that employment of children shall not be allowed to continue, where prohibited. The target of inspections, prosecutions and claim cases will have to be achieved for every year of the project.

Income and Employment Generation

The importance of employment and income-generating scheme in any child labour project need hardly be stressed. Indeed, they are fundamental to the achievement of the second objective of the project, namely the reduction in the incidence of child labour through an overall improvement in the soci-economic status of the families or the child workers impoves, there will be less need for the child to go out to earn.

A number of employment and income generation programmes of the Government are in opration at present throughout the country. These are: the Integrated Rural Development Programme (IRDP), the National Rural Employment Programme (NREP), the Rural Landless Employment Guarantee Programme (RLEGP), the Development of Women and Children in Rural Areas (DWACRA), the Self-Employment Programme for the Urban Poor (SEPUP), etc. The project management will make efforts to get as many child labour families as possible covered under the ongoing poverty amelioration schemes.

As the project management will themselves not be

administering these programmes, their role will be more that of catalyst. However, each of these programmes has its own parameters and constraints. It is, therefore, possible that despite efforts all child labour families may not be coverd under the existing poverty amelioration programmes of the State and Central Governments. Additional funds are therefore, proposed to be provided under this project to cover child labour families under poverty amelioration schemes similar to those of the IRDP. As in the case of IRdP, the assistance will be partly in the shape of a bank loan at low interest rates and partly in the shape of subsidy. The same kind of economic assets provided under the IRDP scheme will be provided under this.

Efforts will also be made to start industries, which are labour-intensive but do not require much capital. In these industries, employment will be given predominantly to family members of child workers.

Since the principal objective of the project is to remove child labour, it will be necessary for the project management to ensure that every family which is given a benefit under this project, removes its child/children from the industry and puts him/her in school. This has to be strictly enforced.

Non-formal Education

Most of the children working in the industry are either dropouts from schools or have never been to school at all. Under the project, non-formal education will be made available to these children.

An essential purpose of non-formal education would be to impart literacy skills of primary education level in order that these children may be able to benefit from other sources of knowledge and information in their later life.

Under the New Education Policy, the Department of Education, Government of India has certain programmes for non-formal education. Non-formal education programmes for working children in areas with a concentration of child labour are also specifically mentioned. Under the scheme of the Department of Education, the Central Government will give financial assistance to the extent of 50% for starting non-formal education centres. Where the centres are for girls, 90% assistance will be given by the Central Government. These programmes will be utilised in the project area as far as possible to give non-formal educaiton to the children engaged in the brassware industry.

Various localities which have a high concentration of child labour have been identified, 18 basic primary schools, whose names are given in Annexure-I have been selected in these areas for providing non-formal education. One hundred children will be taught in each school in two fours-the first batch from 1.00 p.m. to 3.00 p.m. and the second from 3.00 p.m. to 5.00 p.m. every day. The Project Director will, in consultation with the Director of Education, draw up the proposals for these non-formal education centres and submit them to the Department of Education, Ministry of Human Resource Development, Government of India, for release of funds.

Monthly evaluation of hte progress of the child will be made by a Committee consisting of selected heads of schools and class teachers with the Project Director acting as the Chairman and Convener of the meetings. The record of evaluation and the suggestions given for improvement will be kept by the Project Director. These non-formal education centres may be named Bal Shramik Vidyapeeths.

Non-formal education is also proposed to be given through special schools under the project. In these schools emphasis will be laid not only on non-formal education but on vocational training, health care, nutrition, recreation as well as on any other needs of the children that might emerge. These schools will be run by voluntary organisations will be identified by the Project Officer and the proposals will be forwarded through him to the Minister of Labour. A hundred per cent financial assistance for these special schools will be given by the Central Government (Ministery of Labour) under this project. Like the other non-formal education centres (assisted by the Deptt. of Education), these special schools will also have to function during working hours. A provision has been made in the project budget to give stipends to the children who attend the special schools. This has been done so as to compensate the children for their loss in earnings as a result of giving up employment.

Vocational Training

Vocational training would be available to the children between the age group of 12 to 14 years. In the first year 90 children may be trained in 30 different units. For this 3 si[ervisors will be required to oversee the training and to ensure that the children are nto otherwise exploited by the employers. The object of the vocational training is to teach the children traditional skills of brassware manufacture at Moradabad. To encourage children to take up vocational training, they will be provided with a stipend of Rs. 100 to Rs. 150 per month.

The training shall be given in selected trades such as engraving, polishing, foundry, gas welding, packing, soldering, electroplating, machining, turnig, etc. Children selected for training will be in the groups of 12 to 14 years. It will be ensured that all these children get education as well.

Health

It is usually found that the health state of child workers is inferior to that of non-working, school-going children. Therefore, providing for health care is sen as an essential component of this project. Efforts will be made to get the School Health Progamme which covers school children in the formal school system to cover the children in the non-formal educaiton centres also.

In addition the special school to be set up will have a specific health care component consisting of medical chick-ups, treatment, maintenance of health hastory sheets, etc.

Conditions of Work and Terms of Employment

While the enforcement of the law is necessary to ensure that children below 14 years do not work in the industry, at the same time conditions in the industry will have to be created so that it is no longer profitable for the employer to engaged child labour. In addition to this, since many of hte parents of child workers are also employed in the industry, improvement of conditions and terms of employment in the industry will have a direct impact on the child workers. The most important step that needs to be taken in this direction relates to wages. Wages should be fixed at a sufficiently high rate to ensure a reasonable income to the workers. Presently, under the Minimum Wages Act, 1948 children between the age groups of 14 to 16 years are paid wages at the rate of two-thirds of the wages admissible to adults. Efforts will be made by Labour Department, Uttar Pradesh to revise minimum wages at par with adults. If it is not possible, wages to children above 14 years should not be less than three-fourths of wages payable to adults. Economically and technologically feasible improvements in the working environment and improvemtns in the manner in which work is designed and organised will be identified. The Directorate General of Factory Advise, Service and Labour Institute, Bombay (under the Ministry of Laobur) will examine defects in lighting, ventilation, etc. in the work palce and suggest corrective measures.

Raising General Consciousness

Efforts will be made through voluntary organisations to raise public awareness regarding the problems of child labour. Camps/Workers can be held and the Radio and TV network utilised. The Central Board for Worker's Education should also be used for conscopismess raising. In the adult education classes run by the Government as well as by non-Governmental organisations, efforts will be made to drive home the Government's message regarding child labour.

Survey

In order to assess the impact, it will be necessary to take up a proper base-line survey to arrive at the actual number of child workers and collect certain infomation about them. According to preliminary estimates the number of children engaged in the brassware industry is approximately 7,500. The majority of the children are boys.

The evaluatory studies will be taken up to assess the progress made towards achieving the objectives indicated. A financial provision has been made in the project budget for this purpose.

5

Why Children work in the Brass Ware Industry

The job of the moulder is a very delicate operation and if there is a slight mistake or accident the boy can get very badly injured and can even lose his limbs. He wears no protective gear and stands barefoot on top of the furnace to either put in the crucible or to remove it. The temperature in the furnace is about 1100 C. As one exporter/manufacturer, explaining the processes in his factory, said: 'See how dexterous this young child is. He has to be. Because even if a drop of molten brass fall on his foot there will be a hole in it.'

THE BRASS WARE INDUSTRY OF MORADABAD UTTAR PRADESH

Moradabad is one of the most important centres of production of art metal wares in the country. It is the district headquarters of the district of the same name in the State of Uttar Pradesh and is situated about a hundred miles from

Delhi on the right bank of the river Ramganga. Flower vases, planters, plates, dinner services, tea sets and various decorative object d'art are all made here.

The history of the brass industry of Moradabad is lost in antiquity. According to the Moradabad Gazetter, the original method of moulding was the para method by which earthen moulds were used to give shape to molten metal. After 1920, the darja (box moulding) system was adopted but only for small articles like handles and spouts. Cutlery began to be manufactured around 1925 and power began to be used towards the end of 1930. Imported brass sheets were used as raw material in the manufacture of utensils but as they were in short supply around 1940,the production of sheets from scrap, virgin copper and zinc was taken up locally.

In 1947, there were only three big exporters in Moradabad: Lala Bhukan Saran, Mousin Yaar Khan and Haji Kallan. After 1947, when there was large-scale migration from Punjab to Moradabad and other cities, the Punjabi Hindus saw the industry as a good investment and began sending samples abroad for orders.

As the industry developed, many outsiders came to settle down in Moradabad. They would get things made by the multiprocess unit manufacturers who were known as Karkhanedars (owner of a karkhana or factory). Many of the local Muslim elite also realized the potential of this business and began exporting goods. Haji Mohammad Jan Mohammad Dawood, who now have almost eight firms, and Haji Mohammad Jikaria Mohammad Yahiya, who also have several firms of exporters, are amongst the earliest ones.

After 1970, a new process of sheet work was introduced and this was done on lathes. Goods like planters began to be manufactured in this fashion which did not require a high level of skill. These goods were made in factories and a large number of the unemployed rural poor came to the city to work there.

The term 'art metal ware', though not very precisely defined, is generally used to denote metal articles which have a higher input of 'artistic skill' as compared to functional household metal wares. More than 90 per cent of the goods produced in Moradabad are exported.

There are almost 150,000 workers engaged directly in the metal ware industry. This figure would include manufacturers, suppliers, exporters and administrative staff. Of the total workers, approximately 40,000-45,000 are children below the age of fourteen years. The basis of the figures of the numbers of workers, both adults and children, has been discussed in detail later.

While the figure of 150,000 workers is an estimate for the metal ware industry. This study was primarily of the brassware industry. It is however very difficult to differentiate between the two as many of the goods made in a particular unit may be for both metal ware and art-metal ware, for the sake of consistency, the industry will henceforth be referred to as the brass ware industry.

Common items produced are flower vases, planter, wall-plates,candle-stands,dinner services, cutlery and so on. The estimated turn-over of the Moradabad brass ware industry for 1986-7 has been Rs. 90 crores (Rs 1 crores is equivalent to Rs 10,000,000) and was likely to cross Rs 100 crores (U.P.State Brass Ware Corporation:Personal Communication). Other important art metal ware centres in Uttar Pradesh are located in Varanasi, Jalesar and Almora.

There are several categories of manufacturing units in Moradabad. Some of the largest units-both in terms of size and in the number of workers employed-will be referred to as factories. At the next level are smaller manufacturing units,where more than one process is carried out-and these are known as karkhanas the literal translation of which is factory. The owner of karkhana is known as a karkhanedar. The term karkhanedar is also used to describe a contractor because many owners of multi-process or double-process units also act as middlemen for procuring items not made by them,from others. At the bottom level are single-process units also act as middlemen for procuring items not made by them, from others. At the bottom level are the single-process workshops referred to as artisan units. While there are a large number of factories,most of the business is in the hands of the middle-level entrepreneur who both employs artisans directly in his multiprocess unit, gets work done by them and supplies the goods to exporters (IDS 1983:11). In some cases, factories do not get all the processes done in their own premises but place orders directly with multi-process unit owners, the karkhanedars. For the sake of simplicity, the term factory or factory owner will be used for those units or owners of units which are very large both in size and in numbers or workers employed on the same premises. The term multi-process unit will be used to refer to karkhanas and the term workshop for single-process units.

It is difficult to give authentic information about the number of establishments working in Moradabad. If a particular unit wishes to avail itself of concessions and facilities given by the government, it has to be registered with the District Industries Centre (DIC). According to the DIC, there were 3000 units registered with them as small-scale units with a capital of less than Rs 35,00,000. But many people this researcher spoke to said there were at least another 3000 units which were unregistered. According to the Factories Act, any unit employing more than twenty workers and not using power or more than nine workers using power is considered a factory. Once the unit is registered as a factory, its workers become entitled to certain rights under the Act. These rights include Employees State Insurance, Provident Fund, leave with pay and so on. Only 381 units were registered as factories and everybody agreed that this was a gross underestimation because employers were chary of becoming legally liable to provide statutory benefits to workers. It will be seen, therefore, that the statistics regarding the number of establishments and factories are quite misleading.

More than 90 per cent of the goods produced in Moradabad are meant for export and this explains the dominant role of the exporter in the industry. Exporters are of two types:manufacturing exporters are few in number and are those who have very large businesses.

Exporters who have entered the field of manufacturing have done so in order to maintain quality control and to preserve the secrecy of their designs. They directly employ few workers themselves and these are either supervisory staff or artisans with a high degree of skills. Their modus operandi is to have a number of captive multi-process units, who use their building space and machinery on the payment of rent. By this means,the manufacturer exporter is sure that his work will be done according to schedule but he has no direct responsibility for or relationship with the workers in these captive units. These workers are the employees of the multi-process unit owner, who usually works on the machines himself as well. Though the building and machinery belong to the manufacturing exporter, it is for the multi-process unit owner to organize his supplies of raw materials like black powder, chemicals and coal and with the help of hired-labour, complete the job contracted out to him. In this type of arrangement, it was also found that many of the units in the premises of the manufacturer exporter were single-process units specializing in particular activities like moulding, scraping, welding, polishing and electroplating.

The non-manufacturing exporter is the more representative figure and accounts for a larger share of the business. His way of working is to ask a multi-process unit owner to give a sample and then place an order after tendering that sample to a number of possible competitors. Scraping, welding, and grinding (fine scraping) are activities commonly carried out in these multi-process units. It is rare for the processes of moulding, polishing and electroplating to be carried out in these multi-process units for these jobs require separate space as they generate a great deal of heat and pollution. The multi-process unit owner is charged with the responsibility not only of completing the processes which he himself carries out in his unit but usually also of getting the goods finished in other respects through different single-process units or workshops.

It will be seen from the above description that the multi process unit owners, who are given orders by the non-manufacturing exporters differ significantly from the multi-process unit owners who are tied to the manufacturing exporters. The former have their own buildings and machinery and are not necessarily linked to a particular exporter. Besides, they operate on a wide canvas and normally get the wares readied in all respects for the exporter. While the multi-process unit owner is an artisan-turned-entrepreneur, the single-process unit owner attached to the manufacturing exporter is more commonly a worker, with a high degree of initiative but who does not perform full-blown entrepreneurial functions.

It was found that of the exporters,75 per cent were Hindus and 25 per cent were Muslims. The Hindus were either Punjabi's who went to Moradabad after Partition or Banias, local trading castes. Punjabi Mussalmans, Ansaris and members of the Khan clan made up the Muslim exporters. As regards the multi-process unit manufacturers, about 65 per cent of them are Muslims (Ansaris, Mansooris, Ghosis, etc.) and 35 per cent are Hindus (mainly Punjabis). Most Hindus labourers belong to lower castes like Bagvans, Balmikis, Lodhas and Ahirs. Amongst the Muslims, the poorer Ansari and Quarishi families work as labourers. While the bulk of the Muslim work force is to be found in small workshops, the majority of Hindu workers are engaged in the large factories.

METHODOLOGY AND FIELDWORK

Data for this study were collected over a period of nineteen days on two separate field trips to Moradabad and its surrounding villages. During these visits,opportunity was taken to hold frank and participatory discussions (where possible) with workers, entrepreneurs, exporters, contractors, and others connected with the trade. An addition, there were interviews with government officials, doctors, social activists and others. During the period of field-work, I spoke to about 300 people belonging to different categories for varying lengths of time.

I visited fifteen large factories. They were large in terms of size of premises and by number of workers employed, who ranged between more than twenty and up to about seventy-five. Visits to the first few factories helped me understand processes of manufacture, and, later I began discussing issues with the factory owner or his representative. Access was made possible since a helpful government official accompanied me. But it was evident that the absence of a questionnaire creates suspicion amongst some factory owners; in particular,those who were exporters or their employees were most reluctant to part with information. However, several factory owners-who were not exporters but supplied them with goods-spoke freely to me for they felt that government gave undue concessions to exporters and did not treat simple manufacturers with the same solicitude. Though the number of large factories visited was relatively small,they took up a disproportionate share of my time as they were dispersed in different parts of the town and had a large number of processes in operation.

I was able to visit some thirty medium-size multi-process units in which the number of processes were limited and less sophisticated as compared to those in the larger factories refer to above. Here I received cordial treatment almost uniformly. These units fell under the jurisdiction of the official accompanying me which was of great advantage for my work. Except for the odd child, children were not found working either in the larger factories or in the medium-sized ones. In many of the units I went to, I could disarmingly that a lower number of worker is reported in order to evade the provisions under the Factories Act that call for certain facilities to be given to worker if the unit is deemed to be a factory.

I saw about a thousand single-process workshops in the by-lanes of Moradabad, away from the main road. This statement needs clarification. These workshops are involved with the processes of moulding ,polishing,scraping,welding, engraving and colouring. Of all these small workshops I saw, more than half were moulding units. Most of the workshops I saw had three or four workers, adults and children. Usually, these small workshops were closed off on three sides and faced the streets for the natural light and ventilation they offered. Commonly, these spaces were part or extensions of the residential complex but clearly demarcated. However, there were also some larger sheds where several adults and children were working in separate units with their own equipment but sharing common space.

Out of nineteen days of fieldwork, twelve days were spent walking through these populated Muslim localities, observing what was going, on spending a few minutes and sometimes engaging there in long conversations with the local people. The purpose of this exercise was to gain a representative understanding of what could be considered the most common form of industrial activity in Moradabad in which the largest number of people are employed, particularly children. One question that I invariably asked was whether the children working in these workshops were part of the families of the adults working there. And this I did by asking the children present what their fathers did and the adults about where their children were and what they did. I shall return later to this theme of children working as hired labour-for it is my contention that official policy rests importantly upon the belief that children in the brass ware industry work along with their families and learn traditional skills.

Since I was there for many days and visited the same localities again and again, sometimes people would offer to take me to their workshops which were in their own homes. I then got the opportunity to see what kinds of units people were running at home. These visits also gave me the chance to talk to people at length-particularly women and girls-who were otherwise invisible. I learnt about the history and development of the industry and the situation of the labour force from older people and others who were not currently employed and involved directly in the industry. Very rarely did the children speak in the presence of adults and it was not possible to get to know what they felt about their work. The children would either listen to what the adults were saying or, if they were asked a direct question, would answer in monosyllables and then lapse into silence. Invariably when a question was asked of a child,an adult would answer. In units where the largest number of children were working-the moulding units-it was risky to ask children questions because of the hazardous nature of the work. Concentrations interrupted might have led to accidents!

One day, leaving early in the morning,I visited six villages within the radius of ten kilometers from Moradabad town. Inspite of the fact that it was so early in the morning, both adults and children were getting ready to leave for the day's work. I had an opportunity to discuss with many mothers and their neighbors the social and economic conditions they lived in and was able to get information about the castes and communities they belonged to.

PROCESSES IN THE MANUFACTURE OF BRASS WARE

There are several processes involved in the manufacture of brass ware. The basic raw material used are copper and Zinc. The making of ingots and sheets is the first stage of the production process. Ingots can be of two types: silli (oblong) and gulli (round). Oblong or round ingots or brass sheets are used depending upon the type of article to be produced.

There are very few factories where ingots are made and these factories supply the other manufacturing units. Copper, zinc and scrap material are put into large graphite crucibles and heated to high temperatures. The resultant molten metal (brass) is then poured into smaller earthenware mould to make the ingots. The shape of the mould is either oblong or round depending on whether oblong or round ingots are being made. Only adults are involved in the manufacture of ingots.

The oblong ingots are sold directly to the darja bhattis (box mould furnaces) in which the worker moulds the various parts of the final product-for example, handles, spouts and lids-as well as small bowls,plates and so on. He breaks off as much of the oblong ingot as necessary, melts it and fashions his goods.

In the box mould furnaces, the following operation are undertaken continuously. The mould or die is put into the box and packed with a black powder made up of sand, clay, oil, molasses and borax and sprinkled with a mixture of ammonium chloride. Apiece of the oblong ingot is put into the graphite crucible and when heated, the molten metal is poured through a spout into the box. The metal solidifies almost immediately into the required shape and the box is then opened to remove the article with a pair of tongs. The mixture of black powder falls out and is then beaten up by hand in preparation for further use. This process is then repeated. Children are used here to rotate the cycle wheel and fans the furnace, to put the ingot into the crucible and heat it, to remove the crucible containing molten brass and hand it to the adult worker and to grind the black powder for re-use.

Round ingots are not sold in that form. In the factories where they are made, they are put onto rolling machines and pressed into sheets of the required specifications. Both round ingots and the sheets that they are fashioned into are manufactured according to the requirements of the indenter. Bowls and plates are examples of the type of goods which have a circular or spherical shape that are made from round ingots.

Apart from oblong and round ingots, the third possible starting point in the production chain is brass sheets. Here, children are not employed. These sheets are mainly manufactured by the Uttar Pradesh State Brass Ware Corporation and then supplied to the manufacturers of brass ware. The goods that are to be made from these sheets are not moulded. The most important item made from these sheets is the planter. The sheets are pressed in factories and given shape and design on electrically operated machines which have dies in them. These planters or pots are moved several times between the press and the furnace before they are given a final shape. They are then scraped by adults on power-operated lathes. In this semifinished form the goods are normally sent to other multi-process manufacturing units, which specialize in the processes of polishing,soldering, electroplating and so on. Goods like planters, which are one of the most important export items, sometimes need ancillary parts like handles and chains, which are manufactured in box mould furnaces and later joined.

When the article in question reaches the stage of being given a shape-whether the starting point be oblong or round ingot or brass sheet-the processes to follow are by and large common, for example, all semi-finished goods are scraped,welded, polished and electroplated or silver-plated. Some wares are engraved and coloured as well.

Semi-finished articles are to be scraped in order to make them smooth and iron out the rough edges. Scraping can be done either by hand or by machine. When it is manual, this involves the used of chisel and hammer. Mechanical scraping, which involves the fixing of the articles on moving rods, is done only by adults in the case or larger wares but young boys can also be found doing this work for smaller pieces.

Welding can be done in three ways:using small furnaces stoves or gas cylinder. Children are engaged in large numbers in welding workshops and their main job is to hold the pieces together which are to be welded. Young women and girls the metal wires around the parts to be welded in their homes an send them to the workshops for welding.

Once the semi-processes goods are scraped and welded, they are then to be washed and polished to give them the requisite gloss. Washing is done in a mixture which has hydrochloric acid and this work is unusually done by children. The article is first cleaned, polishing by machine involves mounting the piece on a spindle or lathe with polishing paint the revolving article as a result of which it gets the required finish;if they are plain, they are polished on machines rotating faster and using discs covered with emery powder. Polishing machines are also called buffing machines.

Engraving is the cutting of a design into the surface of a metal. The engraver cuts the required design on the ware with the help of engraving tools and light weight hammer. In the case of ordinary work, the design can be carved by the engraver from memory. If the design are intricate, the design are the first drawn on paper and outlined on the ware. After engraving, the resultant depressions are filled with shellac by heating the articles and applying shellac sticks. The articles are then glazed by rubbing with wood ash. Children and women are also engraved in this work. The main raw materials used are shellac, lacquer, colours, thinners, soft coke and zinc oxide. Frequently, goods are polished both before and after engraving.

Though not all wares electroplated or silver-plated, when they are, it is the last stage in the production process. The purpose of this activity is to prevent or postpone the tarnishing of wares. It involves tying the goods on metal wires and then immersing them in baths of a solution containing potassium cyanide and silver nitrate while and electric current is passed. The next step is to cover them in ammonium chloride powder, which absorbs moisture and hastens drying. Children are to be found both in the activities of tying these articles to the wires and covering them with ammonium chloride powder.

It has been reported that till the late 1950s or early 60s,89 per cent of all establishments in Moradabad worked without power with only 11 per cent using power. The establishments using power were engaged mainly in scraping, electroplating and polishing. Today, many item, particularly those made from brass sheets, are made by using mechanized methods. The large units have facilities for mechanical rolling cutting and fabricating pressed sheets articles. There is still no mechanization in sheet beating, casting, engraving and enameling, but more and more units are introducing a low level of mechanization in the processes of sheet work, soldering and scraping.

CHANGES IN DEMAND:IMPACT UPON TECHNOLOGY, LABOUR AND STRUCTURE

There was time about twenty-five or thirty years ago when the brass ware industry was entirely a cottage industry in which the artisan worked with the help on his family labour an virtually no hired help. I was told that the goods produced at that time were vases, decanter, wine glasses, decorative plates and the like. Though there was a small export market in the Middle East, most of the goods made were sold in India. The designs that were carved, the colours that were used and the wares that were thus made-all bore the unmistakable stamp of Moradabad and made that town famous for its particular type of brass ware. The skilled craftsman was in control of the industry to the extent that he purchased the raw materials himself, fashioned the goods and then sold them. Since there was a specialization in different types of skills, processes that could not be done at home were got done by other artisans.

The self-employed artisan of your, who was the representative figure in the production system until a few years ago, is now conspicuous by his substantially reduced presence. In 1959-60, it was estimated that 66 per cent of workers were self-employed . By 1974, the proportion of self-employed workers was estimated at less than 1 per cent (IDS) 1983:29). This was not an isolated development.

The kinds of changes that have taken place in the organization of production of the brass ware industry of Moradabad have been well analyzed in a study on the subject undertaken by the Industrial Development Service (IDS). It will be useful to quote here at length from the report.

There has been a an organizational change in terms of (i) and increase in the average number of workers per establishment....(ii) and increase in the number of multi-process establishments (karkhanas) (iii) decline in the category of workers described as 'self-employed" (iv) an increase in the number of manufacturers, suppliers and exporters who co-ordinate the completion of a number of operation through different sets of artisans. This is reflected in the shift in the ownership of working capital. In 1979-80 exporters accounted for 67 per cent of the working capital employed, while the other 33 per cent was accounted for by suppliers and manufacturers. Even allowing for a margin of error or a definitional discrepancy, it supports the decline in the self decline in the self-employed category and an increase in the proportion of wage earners among the craftsmen (ibid.:5-6).

What accounts for these changes? Earlier, even though art-ware always earmarked for export, there was an important domestic market for brass utensils. Rises in the prices of raw material, the difficulty of keeping brass utensils from tarnishing and the growing popularity of stainless steel gradually eroded the domestic market. At the same time, there were significant changes in the nature and scale of demand from international markets in the USA and Europe.

Planter, dinner plates, tea services and other items of table-ware were sought for in international markets. These were not the traditional brass ware item made in Moradabad like flower vases, decanters, wine glasses, decorative table tops and so on. The traditional methods of manufacturer of the traditional items of brass ware which I have described earlier in Chapter1 consisted of a series of operations being performed by a particular manufacturer such as, moulding in box moulds, welding, scraping, polishing, engraving and colouring. The technology thus employed was not suitable for mass production and mass production was called for by the new, enormous scale of international demand. Moreover, the kinds of goods that found a market abroad were such that they lent themselves to the technology of mass production.

Planters,dinner services, bowls and so on could be manufactured by machines on which there were dies containing designs which were impressed upon large numbers of pieces simultaneously. Factories manufacturing sheets of different specifications sprang up in response to the new climate of demand and such sheets could now be ordered by other entrepreneurs according to their needs. The introduction of mechanization in the production of brass sheets made the procurement of this raw material much easier for the entrepreneur. It can thus be seen how the change in the quality and scale of demand was importantly responsible for the changes in technology that followed.

I have earlier drawn attention to the fact that the traditional methods of manufacture required artisans who had skills in particular areas such as moulding, engraving, scraping an polishing. With the advent of mechanization, certain skills became redundant. Scraping and polishing which were traditional female preserves were now done by machine. As a result, female workers were displaced in large number. In a later section, the situation of the female worker will be accused in greater detail. Moulders still have an important role to play because they mould all the new technology. Engravers, on the other hand, have suffered a substantial set-back for they have role in the new technological processes and there is little demand for traditional carvings.

The growth of the industry created a demand for a large work-force and this demand was met by workers from the rural areas of Moradabad and from Bihar and eastern Uttar Pradesh. The level of mechanization is not particularly advanced: unskilled and semi-skilled workers are quite capable of handling the machines currently used. This is an additional reason for the changed profile of the brass ware worker as be becomes transformed from being a skilled artisan to a wage labourer.

The children of artisans,it would be safe to say, were always involved with work of their fathers and mothers whether on a part-time or full-time basis. But such a situation obtained when the industry had a primarily cottage character. A combination of factors resulted in significant change. The prices of raw materials rose, there was a change in the nature and scale of demand, mechanization was introduced and women were displaced. Together,these events resulted in a substantial increase in the share of children in the work force though this did not occur in a uniform way. For example, in the larger factories of Moradabad, it was observed that there were virtually no children at all. When I asked factory-owners why this was so,they offered two reasons. The first and more important one, which seemed convincing to me when I saw the machines involved, was that the new technology was not suitable for the height and strength of children. The size of the machine and the nature of the process involved such as, removing the round ingots from the furnace, pressing them into shape, re-heating and pressing the unfinished wares several-times, seemed to be beyond the physical capacity of children. The other reason proffered by factory owners was that child labour was banned under the Factories Act and they would not want to risk prosecution or harassment on that account. Of course,it was easier for labour inspectors to inspect the comparatively fewer factories there are than the innumerable workshops. Yet, I felt that what the factory owner was doing was rational from his point of view in that it was not worth his while to employ children when the new technology was conducive to the use of adults rather than children, and the use of children would not yield economic advantage. Furthermore, factory owners would sub-contract the jobs of moulding, polishing and electroplating to workshops in which child labour was freely used and abused without attracting any legal liability for doing so.

Even if it is true that children are hardly employed in factories, nevertheless they are employed in most multi-processes such as moulding, welding, polishing, scraping and electroplating. The main explanation for the use of children in these processes lies in the fact that, apart from it being feasible to do so, children are paid less than adults and hence production costs are kept relatively low.

I shall now look at how the changed demand for brass ware has affected the structure of the industry. The relatively self-contained skilled artisan of yesteryear is no longer an important factor in the production process. The IDS study, referred to earlier in this section, points out how between 1959-60 and 1974 the proportion of self-employed persons dropped from 66 per cent to less than 1 per cent. The export market has increased the importance of entrepreneurial functions. There has been thus a shift in the pattern of ownership and control from the self-employed artisan to the entrepreneur or multi-process unit owner and middleman. In the late 1950s,the general pattern was that either the artisan worked in his own house, or in a room attached to his house but clearly for work purposes, or several artisans jointly rented a common shed. But today, there has been a shift in the pattern of ownership in the sense that those working in common sheds are more likely to wage earners under one establishment or karkhana rather than several individuals sharing the common space.

It is clear, therefore that the category of self-employed artisans, who work for themselves with an investment in fixed and working capital, has virtually disappeared. Most artisans have reduced to wage labourers even though outwardly the industry may retain the nature and structure of cottage industry.

It will be evident from the above that the most important factors in the changes that have taken place with respect to technology, the labour force and structure of the industry has been the qualitative and quantitative change in the international demand for the products of Moradabad.

EMPLOYMENT, WAGES AND CONDITIONS OF WORK

I have referred earlier to the importance of the brass ware industry form the point of view of employment in Moradabad. Both governmental and non-governmental sources estimated that at least three-fourths of the population of the city was dependent for their livelihood on industry. At least 150,000 people could be said to be engaged in the metal ware industry and many more are employed indirectly. though most workers were employed on a full-time basis, about 20 per cent of them are from the rural areas. The latter work during the slack periods of agricultural activity and are usually not available during the sowing and harvesting seasons.

In 1980, there were communal riots in Moradabad that claimed several lives and much property. The aftermath of the riots was a climate of distrust and uncertainty and long-lasting tension. Export order could not be met in the time and there was a slump in the industry leading to high levels of unemployment. Other countries stepped in when India failed to supply its goods. And the impact of the riots could still be felt till as late as 1985. The long period of economic insecurity has conditioned the way in which worker look upon the industry: today they are grateful for the work that they have and concentrate their energies upon earning a living. The absence of other employment opportunities makes the workers wholly dependent upon the metal ware industry. Militancy and a trade union movement are both conspicuous by their absence.

When we look at the religious composition of the workers, it is apparent that those who work in big factories and large multi-process units are mainly Hindus and those who are employed in the smaller units are almost entirely Muslim. This is partly to do with the fact that the smaller units are located in the city centre which are Muslim dominated areas and where Hindu men are not encouraged because of the tradition of purdah (the seclusion of women). Moradabad is one of the few cities in India where Muslims outnumber Hindus.

Today, when business is thriving, there is hardly any unemployment for male worker in Moradabad. I was told that most people-excluding women-were assured of at least 200-250 days of work in a year. Most workers interviewed said that they could earn about Rs 400 to Rs 500 a month and nobody even referred to the minimum wages fixed for the industry as these were fixed many years ago and were much less than the prevailing wage rates.

In the last twenty years or so with the increasing demand for labour, there has been a large and growing component of migratory labour from the adjoining villages. Every morning, workers come from villages like Macheria, Hartala, Menather, Uchangaon, Langada, Betiyan, Majola, Khadakpur, Mulak,Kalyanpur, Dhakka, Jayantipur,etc. Those who own cycles, cycle to work. Early in the morning, the streets of Moradabad are packed with workers going to factories. Double Phatak is the area where workers can be sent at 7.45 in the morning either walking or cycling to work. The Amroha passenger train mainly carries workers from the more distant villages to work in the brass ware industry of Moradabad. These are, by and large, landless labourers or people with a little land and belonging to the Scheduled Case communities or they are Muslims. There is also now a very large component of Bihari labour.

Labour workers complain that their situation has worsened as a result of the entry of labourers from the rural areas and, in particular, because of those who have migrated from Bihar. For the Bihari workers and those coming from parts of eastern Uttar Pradesh, the brass ware industry has been a boon. The wages paid to them, even though lower than those paid to local people, are more than what they would have got in their own areas, Both these categories of workers, they felt, depressed the wages in the market as they were prepared to work for less. It was interesting to find in Moradabad that the wages paid to workers depended at least in part on whether they were city people, rural labour or migrant Biharis, the latter two categories being willing to settle for less. Conversations with factory in demand because they were the cheapest and always available. People coming from the adjoining villages were considered unreliable because they would stay away from work during peak agricultural seasons and city labourers were thought to be arrogant.

Three modes of payment are to be found in the industry:salaries, daily wages and piece-rate. The number of salaried employees is negligible both in absolute terms and as proportion of the work-force. Wherever it is possible to quantify the work to be done, wages are paid according to the piece-rate system. And where it is not feasible, people are on daily wages. For example, the moulder in a box mould furnace workshop was paid according to the amount of brass moulded. Polishers and electroplating workers were paid daily wages. Engravers and those who coloured the designs were paid piece-rate wages. Other workers who did miscellaneous jobs like fetching and carrying and are helpers were all on daily wages.

Most workers I spoke to had to work at least ten to eleven hours a day. When large export orders had to be met by deadlines, people would work through the night as well. Over-time would be paid for the extra hours of work put in and workers had no complaint about their long hours of work or about working at nights; they did not consider themselves to be exploited. The power supply in Moradabad being erratic and uncertain, workers would often spend hours just waiting for it and then work into the night as well in order to earn a minimum amount of money. In this respect, workers in the bigger factories were better off since there would be generators installed in them. Workers were not paid on days they did not report for duty or the factory was closed. All power-operated industries are supposed to be shut once a week as a measure of power conservation and so, whether they like it or not, workers get unpaid holiday every week.

As mentioned earlier, according to the Factories Act, any unit which uses power and employs more than nine workers or has twenty or more workers nut does not use power is deemed to be a factory and consequently, workers in such units are entitled to various rights like Employees State Insurance, Provident Fund,leave with pay and so on. In the case of a leading exporter, there were more than 500 workers in his four-storied building but the Manager told me that there were only thirty-five workers who were regular employed by contractors. The factory owner did not incur any legal liability on their account although they were producing goods for him with raw materials purchased by him, using his machinery and doing the work in his promises. This situation may be said to be typical of other manufacturer exporters as well.

Two encounters I had are worth recounting for what they tell. In one factory, a worker told me in the presence of the owner that he was deeply indebted to the latter for the factory owner had spent about Rs 2000 on private medical treatment for the worker's wife when she had an accident. He told me in all sincerity that had it not been for the owner's assistance,his wife would have lost an arm. When the worker left, the owner said to me:

I spent this money which I needn't have but I've got the loyalty of this man for life. He is a skilled worker and can supervise new recruits. He will never leave me to work for another man even at a higher wage. He keeps a check on other workers and reduces my burden of work. The money I spent is nothing compared to the returns I get.

One Works Manager said:

If the employer is good, the workers will work well. We pay our workers monthly wages plus commission for production as well as Provident Fund, bonus,leave, Employees State Insurance, etc.People don't realize that if you treat workers well, they will never let you down. Our work is highly skilled. If we did not have permanent workers, we would lose a lot by training new recruits. This way we save money. And since we pay extra for exceeding production targets, the workers work well.

The instances cited above were exceptions and certainly do not exemplify a general trend. But where workers are treated well, there is a clear understanding on the part of the management that such treatment is justifies by the returns it gives.

People engaged in the job of polishing probably had the most harrowing experience in the brass industry. Some polishers said that if they worked continuously for thirty days in the month, they would be dead in two years because the work is so hazardous. For every fifteen days of work, they have to take a break for fifteen days. Employers, however, this as irresponsibility on the part of workers was that they were so unreliable. Electroplates told me that because the job was hazardous, they could not afford to work for more than twenty days in the month. I shall return to this question later.

Another story though not representative needs to be told. In one factory I visited, workers employed in moulding, polishing and scraping were locked up in cages. When the employed took me to visit this part of his factory, the supervisor first unlocked the main grill door. As we entered, there were large rooms with grills on the windows and grilled doors. Each process was being done in a different room and the grilled doors were locked from outside. Since part of the structure was open for light, it was also grilled. There was a small tea-stall inside the premises and whenever workers wanted drinking water or tea, it was passed through the grills. After we left, I noticed the supervisor locking the doors behind us! The exporter explained that these measures were necessary because workers were by and large dishonest and would try and steal the raw material which was almost as expensive as gold!

PARTICIPATION OF CHILDREN IN THE WORK-FORCE

There are no precise figures available for the number of workers in the brass ware industry, whether adults or children. Estimates made by different agencies vary and sometimes quite widely. The District Industries Centre, a government source, estimated that in 1987 out of a total of 16,000 workers,9100 were men,900 were women and 5000 were children. In sharp contrast, a study by Kulshrestha and Sharma in 1980 puts the total labour force at 1,00,000 of which 24 per cent or 24,000 were children (Kulshreshtha and Sharma 1980). Again, a study conducted in 1979-80 by IDS in Moradabad argues that of about 70,000 workers,80-85 per cent are males, 10-15 per cent are children and rest females (IDS-1983:4-5). In other words, there are between 56,000-59,000 men, 7000-10,500 children and the rest are women.

An unpublished report of 1988 of the Labour Department of the Government of Uttar Pradesh refers to the findings of a survey begun in 1981 by the National Industrial Development Corporation (NIDC) and quotes them. These figures do not include registered factories but concentrate on small-scale units. According to the NIDC report (cited in Table III below),of 29,100 workers, 20,370 are men,7566 are children and 1164 are women. Thus, nearly 70 per cent of all workers are men and more than 25 per cent are children.

The same report refers to the conclusions of sample survey carried out in August, 1986, by the Labour Department itself. This survey concluded that while 75 per cent of children work as part of family labour, only 25 per cent of them are wage earners. It went on to estimate that number of such children was between 1800 and 2000 from the point of view of rehabilitation under the National Child Labour Programme (Labour Commissioner, U.P 1988:3). This researcher was told informally that in the absence of adequate staff, less than a hundred families were interviewed.

Table-III

Break-up of Units (Process-wise) of Brass ware Industry atMoradabad

Nature of job	Total No. of units	Men	Women	Children	Total
Shapping	425	1860	23	296	2179
Polishing	1190	4068	284	1387	5651
Casting	2510	6072	276	1872	8220
Welding	431	746	-	18	764
Enamelling	85	712	63	96	871
Scraping	890	4346	386	2193	6925
Electroplating	256	1853	212	1613	3678
Engraving	1560	721	-	91	812
Total	7650	20,370	1164	7566	29100

SOURCE: Labour Commissioner, U.P.: Project Report of Rehabilitation of Child Labour in Brass ware Industry of Moradabad prepared by Labour Commissioner, U.P. January 9 1988,pp.1-2 (unpublished).

The number of children working in the brass ware industry has been thus estimated as 1800-2000 (by the Labour Department), as 5000(by the District Industries Centre), as 7000-10,000 (by the Industrial Development Services report)as 7566 (by the National Industrial Development Corporation report) and as 24,000 (by Kulshreshta and Sharma). Even allowing for natural increase in numbers since the studies relate to different years, such wide variations need to be explained.

When I spoke to different categories of people in Moradabad like entrepreneurs, exporters, workers and others not connected with the government, almost everybody said that about 90 per cent of people in Moradabad worked in the brass ware industry. According to the 1981 Census, the population of Moradabad town was 3,45,350. But when I asked about actual numbers, I was given a range of between 2,00,000 and 3,00,000 people as working the industry. I was also given to understand that more than 25 per cent of the work-force is made up of children, even though the proportion of children varies from process to process. Even if one takes a lower figure of 1,50,000 as the number of workers, it would mean that there are about 40,000-45,000 children working in the industry.

Government reports and government officials tend to severely underestimate the size of the problem. For one thing, no systematic survey has been carried out by them. For another, if the belief is that only 25 per cent of the working children are hired labourers in need of rehabilitation, the size of the problem becomes automatically smaller. But twelve days of seeing and visiting several hundred small units in the by-lanes of Moradabad convinced me that in virtually no case were children working as part of family labour. To the last child, they were all hired by others. It is in the light of my observation of different processes and assessment of the proportions of children in each of them coupled with the discussions I had with a wide cross-section of people in Moradabad that I would estimate the number of workers to be at least, 1,50,000 and the number of workers in different process and the share of children in them have been calculated on a similar basis. Yet, I cannot claim that the figures offered in this report are free of error but am confident they are closer to the facts than official documents allow.

Seventy-five to 80 per cent of the children are Muslims from the town of Moradabad and 20 to 25 per cent Hindus, usually Scheduled Castes, from adjoining villages in a radius of five to six kilometers from the town. The latter can be seen at the railway station in the morning sitting on top of the carriages of the Amroha and Chaumasia passenger trains. The age-range of the child workers is between eight and twelve years. The Bhagvans, Jatavs,Lodhes and Khagis are the castes to which the children normally belong.

I was told by village officials that while adults go on their own in search of work, children are recruited by dalals (middlemen),who usually belong to the village and who get paid a commission for bringing child workers. Thekedars (contractors) and workshop owners prefer children because they are easy to control. The middlemen look out for children. Their parents are offered an advance of Rs 100 or the equivalent of a month's wages. If a parent takes an advance, the child has to work whether he likes it or not. If he plays hookey, the wages of other children from the same village are cut and this way the town itself, their parents are induced into sending them to work by the lure of an advance of say Rs 500. This lump sum payment is a big incentive for parents and it is adjusted against a child's wages over a few months. Unlike as in the case of children in the rural areas, there are no middlemen involved to recruit urban children into the work-force.

MOULDING

Of the 30,000-odd workers involved in moulding in the box mould furnace workshops, about 50 per cent or 15,000 are children below the age of fourteen years. Their main job, as explained earlier, is to rotate the wheel which fans the under-ground furnace. These boys are known as pankhawalas (the person who fan the flames) and this is the first job given to a new child recruit. The ghadiyawala (the person who melts the raw material in the graphite crucible) is the boy who heats the oblong ingot on top of the furnace, breaks it into small pieces with a hammer and melts the required amount of brass. When the molten brass is ready, he lifts the graphite crucible containing the raw material with long tongs and passes it to the adult worker, who then pours it into the moulds. some times. When the adult is holding the mould, he pours the brass into it and then replaces the crucible into the furnace. Often, the job of the boy who rotates the wheel also includes that of removing the crucible from the furnace and vice-versa. Both the boy who rotates the wheel and the boy who removes crucible help grind the hot black mixture into a fine powder with their bare hands and help remove the hot moulded metal from the moulds. These are all continuous processes and if the child is not rotating the wheel, he either removing the crucible or grinding the black powder or removing the hot moulded metal. There is not even a minute's rest in a ten-hour day for a child working at a box mould furnace workshop.

The jobs described above in these workshops are done only by children. Employers justified the use of child labour for these tasks by saying that unless children began this work at an early age, they would never be able to become moulders in their adulthood; a high degree of skill was said to be involved. Yet, I interviewed several adult moulders who had not done such work as children. In fact, in the 600 odd box mould furnace workshops I visited, I found that the moulders were almost always under 30 years of age. People told me that children who work in box furnace workshops from a young age either do not survive as adults or become too ill to work. Tuberculosis (TB) is the most common consequence. In one unit I visited, as I was talking photographs, the child poured the molten metal into the mould and suddenly the room filled with fumes and everybody began to cough. It took me full fifteen minutes to recover from such a brief exposure and these children work in these conditions for ten hours a day, day in and day out! The moulder who employs children knows that his working life in limited and therefore tries to maximize his profits in the short time available to him by hiring children. The other costs of production like coal, sand, molasses, oil, etc., are beyond his control.

POLISHING

The other process in which a large number of children are working is polishing the semi-finished goods. Polishing employs about 25,000 workers of whom about 12,000 are children. Unlike the lock industry where children can be seen working on the buffing machines in large numbers, in the brass ware industry children spend their time applying chemicals on the wares to be polished, dipping wares in acid baths before they are polished, putting masala (a term used for describing a mix of ingredients)-on the buffs so that they could be used again. Many children working in polishing units are from the adjoining villages. I was told that while children working the box mould furnace workshops invariably belonged to the city, children engaged in polishing work often came from outside. It was explained that polishing was a relatively unskilled activity into which untrained recruits could enter, while moulding required some training;living and growing up in the urban environment was supposed to help.

I visited six villages around Moradabad city from which people came to work in the brass ware industry. Dhakka village is five kilometers from Moradabad city. The total population of the village is 2000, of which 250 people go daily to work in the multi-purpose workshop units and about fifty are children below the age of fourteen years and about 150 are adolescents below eighteen years. The work of polishing and moulding is also done in the village and many people work here. All the workers working the village and in the city are Muslims. Kundanpur village has a total population of about 3000. This village is about four kilometers from the city. Most of the workers go to the polishing units in the city. Approximately 250-300 workers commute daily on cycles or walk to work. There are no multi process units in the village so they all work in the city. There are at least 160 children below the age of fourteen years. Most of the children had already left for work when I visited the village at seven in the morning and could come back home only as late as nine at night but sometimes only at eleven. Since they were afraid of walking home alone, they would wait for their friends and then come together. A common sight in the morning is young children holding on to their small tiffin-carriers as they set out to work. None of the children interviewed earned more than Rs 100 a month. The children said they continued to work as long as they were asked to by the unit owner.

Dhimri village is six to seven kilometers from Moradabad with a total population of 5000 people. From this village, only children below the age of fifteen years go to work. Approximately 200 children commute daily. They are either Muslims or Satar by caste and belong to families of landless labourers or people with small amounts of land.

Menather, another village, is five kilometers from the city with a population of 5000 people. About 100 workers commute to work of whom fifty are children. Most of the workers are Muslim. Jayantipur village, which is six kilometers from the city, has a population of 3000. Out of 250 workers who go to work, 150 are children. Many children and adults work in the polishing units set up in the village. While the adults are mainly Bagvan by caste, the children are mainly Muslims. In Bhadora village, about three kilometer from the city, 150 workers go to Moradabad and they are either Bagvans or Muslims. Pandit Nagla is another village about three kilometers from Moradabad. While parents are engaged in agricultural work, children, about 150, go to work. They are either Muslims or belong to the lower castes of Jatav, Lodhe and Khaagi.

Most multi-process unit owners prefer children from the rural areas because they are cheaper than children of the city. Most children working in polishing workshops were in the age-range of twelve to thirteen years, earner about Rs 100 a month and were kept on a monthly salary. The younger children, between the ages of eight and nine, earned Rs 60 a month and their wages were cut and day they did not come to work. The adults were paid on a piece-rate basis. The children who worked with moulders earned Rs 100-150 a month once they had gained experience and reached the age of twelve or thirteen years. Nine or ten years-olds earned Rs 3 a day and still younger seven to nine-years-old earned Rs 60 a month.

No child below the age of fourteen years earned more than Rs 200 a month irrespective of the kind of work he did or the number of hours he worked.

ELECTROPLATING

Out of 20,000 workers engaged in electroplating, about 5000 are children. The main job that children are involved in is in the tying of articles with wires which are then submerged by adults in chemical tanks containing potassium cyanide. Once the goods are plated, the wires are removed also by children and the wares are taken out into the sun by children where they cover each article with ammonium chloride powder so that all the moisture is absorbed. In the evening, the children carry the dried goods inside the workshop.

WELDING

There are probably 10,000 workers engaged in welding, of whom about 7000 are children. It was common in the lanes of Moradabad to see children working as helpers to adults, who were welding. The adult usually wore protective glasses to prevent injury to his eyes but the child, who passed him the goods and watched him carefully, did not use anything at all. The workshops where welding was carried out were very small and there was not enough space for the children to sit. The adult would sit outside the workshop and the children sat inside, often on top of the cylinder because there was not enough space on the workshop floor. If the cylinder exploded, as has sometimes happened, it was the child who would be injured. One other feature of welding workshops was that the number of children was very large per adult. One frequently saw one adult and three or four children in one workshop, though there were also units where there were no one children at all. Children working in welding workshops were very young. Most of the children were in the age-range of six to nine years.

ENGRAVING

A few thousand children work in the processes of engraving designs and colouring. Children involved in these tasks more often than not help their fathers and contribute their mite to the labour of the family. The explanation for this phenomenon is that both engraving and colouring are highly skilled activities which require long periods of training. Parents who want a quick return by way of the child's wage cannot afford to wait the necessary time if their children were to take up these occupations. Because of changes in market demand, engraving and colouring are not at a premium any more and the wages for this category of artisans have in fact fallen. There is no certainty of employment for those who enter these lines. The rest of the workers were employed in factories, etc.

WAGE LABOUR NOT FAMILY LABOUR

Except in the process of engraving and colouring, child labour in the brass ware industry of Moradabad is not a part of family labour as it is usually made out to be. The Child Labour (Prohibition and Regulation) Act of 1986 does not apply to those children who work as part of family labour. In any case, in Moradabad, almost all the children work as wage labour and going by visual impression children do not seem to be remotely related to the adults they work with.

At one box mould furnace workshop in Dhakka village, a man and a boy were working together. I presumed that since this was a village and the work was being done in the courtyard of the house, the man and boy would be related. Since the man was not old enough to be the father of the child, I thought he was the brother and said, 'I suppose he is your brother',pointing to the boy. To which he answered in the affirmative. A little later, while we were waiting for the moulds to be prepared, someone said:

This boy has been working for at least six years. (The boy was about twelve or thirteen years). Even his younger brother works and he is only seven years old. Rasheed is the sole earning member of his family. His father is dead and mother unemployed with lots of little brothers and sisters to support. He now ears Rs 5 a day.

Then I asked,'You mean you two are not related?' This boy is not a brother? He said,' He is not a real brother, but in the vocabulary of the village, everybody is a brother'.

During the course of the study in Moradabad, I visited nearly a 1000 units of different types and found that parents and children worked together in less than ten or fifteen of them. Such detailed investigation is not normally done by inspecting authorities even if they possessed the will and man-power to do so. Hence the myth that most children who work in Moradabad work as part of family labour persists. Exactly the opposite is the case.

ATTITUDES OF PARENTS

I interviewed several parents about their attitudes towards the fact that their children worked. Many times I got the distinct impression that parents believed that children were born to serve and support them and saw nothing wrong in their not being in school or not being able to play. It is, of course, true that few parents could afford to send children to school or let them have the luxury of play. The attitudes of many parents reflected the expectations that society has of children with respect to their roles and, in particular, their filial duties.

When I asked Sunil's mother whether Sunil protested about being made to work, she said: 'If he doesn't work, he will die. We don't have a government job that we can feel him ourselves without lifting a finger. Whatever the earns is spent on him.'

At bara Shah Shafa, Khajoor ki Sarai, Feel Khana and Lal Masjid, there are many polishing workshops. At one that I went to, two boys of twelve and fourteen years were working. The younger one told me that he lives on the premises and cooked his food on an electric stove. The room he lived in was small and most the space was occupied by a wooden bed on which the two boys slept. A section of the room was partitioned and two buffing machines installed. These boys got up at 6 a.m. and by 7 a.m. when I visited, they were busy at work. Alam said that he earned Rs 250 a month and went home once in eight days. He was the sole supporter of his family of six brothers and sisters and a mother. His father, a rickshaw-puller died two years ago, and since then the boy had started working. I was told that most the children who lived on the premises were those who had come from the rural areas. About 10 per cent of all working children lived in the workshops.

HEALTH HAZARDS

The two most hazardous processes in the brass ware industry are moulding and polishing and it is in these two process that child labour is all-pervasive. I saw 600 box mould furnace workshops and this was the recurring pattern. For every adult, there were two children. The work in the box furnace work-shops is extremely dangerous. The child is employed to do two types of jobs. He rotates the wheel which is called a pankha (literally means a fan. In this context it is the rotation of the wheel which is called a pankha to keep the furnace fire burning). In some box mould furnace workshops there were only two workers, an adult and a child. In these workshops, the child would rotate the wheel. After the temperature had reached a certain level, the child tested it by opening the top of the underground furnace and throwing a little powder into it. If the material-molten brass-was ready,blue and green flames would shoot up from the mouth of the furnace. The child then took a large pair of tongs and lifted the crucible of molten brass from the furnace and handed it over to the adult who poured the molten brass into the already prepared moulds. The boy then returned the crucible into the furnace with raw material and helped the adult to open the hot moulds and remove the pieces. As soon as this was done, he and the adult would grind the hot sand till it was very fine. Then,while the moulds were prepared by the adult, the child went back to sit at the wheel to fan the flames.

The job of the moulder is a very delicate operation and if there is a slight mistake or accident the boy can get very badly injured and can even lose his limbs. He wears no protective gear and stands barefoot on top of the furnace to either put in the crucible or to remove it. The temperature in the furnace is about 1100 degree C. As one exporter/ manufacturer,explaining the processes in his factory,said:' See how dexterous this young child is. He has to be. Because even if a drop of molten brass falls on his foot there will be a hole in it.

The child is not only in danger of getting badly burnt but both he and the adult worker inhale the fumes and gases which are let off from the furnace and again when the molten brass is poured into the moulds developed tuberculosis. A local doctor, Anwar Hussain of Peerzada,said that almost every brass-worker suffered from TB or other upper respiratory tract infections after a few years. This could be avoided only if the worker looked after himself and ate well. But since they cannot afford good food, the combination of poor nutrition and bad working conditions reduces the life span of workers by half. No one worked for more than ten or fifteen years and none lived beyond the age of forty years. In fact,in the 600 or so moulding units I visited, the workers were remarkably young!

In Bhurra Mohalla, commonly referred to as Jatavon ka Mohalla, near Prince Road, about 100 families live there and almost 500 people are engaged in polishing work. Some of them polish steel utensils and others polish brass. There are hundreds of polishing machines installed in the locality;most of them are owned by workers who save and after a few years get a machine and then use hired help, mainly child labour. I talked to at least thirty people, many of whom had lost members of their families. Draupadi was a middle-aged woman whose child had started working at the age of eight and died the previous year at the age of twenty-five years. He was a polisher. Mangal Sein is sixty,and works as cobbler. His four adult sons are dead. The youngest died the week before my visit, after vomiting blood. Just across the lane from Draupadi's house, a young adolescent boy had died the night before and the family was taking the body for its last rites. People in Jatavon Ka Mohalla said that 60 percent of them die soon after. A young adolescent boy, Prakash said:' used to work on the machines, but since I started vomiting blood, I hire other workers, mainly children.' being asked why people sent their children to work when they knew that the child would die in any case. If he doesn't work,he will die of starvation in a few days. If he works, then death is at least postponed for a few years.'

Everyone told me that death, and a very painful one at that was inevitable for polishers at a very young age but there was no alternative. Chandrasen said:'What can I say but that every family has lost one or two adolescent boys or adult sons? Now we have started taking this for granted.'

Local doctors admitted that brass-workers were prone to TB but they felt that this was largely due to poverty, malnutrition and congestion in their living quarters. They were not willing to admit easily that these problems were particularly acute for brass-workers, especially those working in box mould furnace workshops and in polishing work. Some reluctantly agreed that there was correlation between work and as even in the city, it was mainly brass-workers who were affected. In the villages where people lived in relatively open spaces, the incidence of TB was negligible but those who were diagnosed as having the disease were brass-workers. In fact, Moradabad is one of the two cities with the highest rate of TB in the state. The local doctors were certainly not in a position to make a distinction between TB and pneumoconiosis or silicosis, the latter being clearly an industrial disease.

Doctors in Moradabad felt that workers who came with chest problems did not get themselves treated. There was such fear in the minds of workers about TB that if their problem was so diagnosed, patients rarely came back even though the disease was curable. This was so partly because the first advice the doctor gave his patient was to change his occupation and to improve his diet. Workers cannot afford to act upon these recommendations.

While local doctors said that the most common medical complaint of workers was chest diseases,workers themselves said that accidents at work were not unusual. Said Rafiqbhai:'Accident are very common. Sometimes, the crucible slips and your hands and feet get badly burnt.

The most hazardous process was considered to be that of moulding in a box mould furnace workshop. One young man, pointing to six children working in his workshop,said:'None of these children will survive beyond the age of thirty. They will die of TB.' Hafizbhai Namunewale said,'Most parents who send their children to work are not even aware of what will happen to the child. They only realize it when a child gets injured and hurt. But by that time, it is too late to repent. And of course. Poverty forces parents to turn a blind eye. If a ghadiya wala drops the ghadiya(crucible),he injures himself will take the hot chimta(tongs) with which the child holds the ghadiya and brand him on the back as punishment! The child will shrivel up in pain and complain to his parents. The mother will put some ointment on the would but will send him right back to work the next day! Ansari Sahib said:

Children who work on polishing machines are at considerable risk. Not only do they inhale all the metal dust and masala, but if a piece,it can severely injure the child. One of the main jobs the children do in polishing units is acid washing of goods before they are polished on buffing machines. You can't enter the room where this is done-all by children. You can actually see the green and blue vapors rising from the acid tubs. We people, who are workers, find it impossible to enter such a room. You won't be able to stand even outside the door. The stench is tremendous and the eyes burn. With polishing the person gets chest diseases. He suffocates to death.

I asked Hafizbhai whether the problem of child labour was better than before or worse. He said:

It's better. At least 5 percent of parents are beginning to realize the harmful effect of work on the child. Look, you can see what happens to the child working as ghadiyawala. His health deteriorates so fast. He is breathing in fumes from the furnace ten to twelve hours a day. Have you been near a darja bhatti? You won't be able to stand there for a few minutes. And this child spends his life in front of it. Within a short time he gets weak. His legs become absolutely skinny. Parents can see this. Every other day the child has fever. It is only desperate parents who sent their child to work at a bhatti(furnace).

Most people interviewed said that accidents were very common amongst children but IO did not see any injured children myself. I was told:

Only when the child is well can he come to work. These days major accidents are relatively few. In the earlier days, when the bhattis used to get scrap as raw material-most of it from the ordinance factories-sometimes whole mohallas used to explode killing adults and children. Now this kind of thing is rare because the raw material is centrally processed at factories which make sillis and gullis and this danger is relatively less.

But in Rasheedbhai's locality just recently, a child was killed and several adults injured in an explosion. In a box mould furnace, a child was breaking up scrap brass from an ordinance factory with a hammer. One of the pieces was a live grenade which exploded on his face. He died instantaneously. But this is rare.

People, particularly local doctors, are reluctant to talk about health hazards to strangers for fear that they will get into trouble for not reporting obvious medico-legal cases. Parents to not talk about them for other reasons. Khalid Begum said:If the poor think of ill-health and illness, how can they work? Accidents are very common. My son lost four fingers. He was under treatment for a long time . Now he's alright.Ruksana Begum had also joined the conversation. She said:

Only a few months back,Mumtaz's fifteen-year old son dies. He had just started working as a welder with a stove welding workshop. God knows what happened, but there was too much gas in the stove and it burst. The boy caught fire and he died before he could be given any medical attention.

Suraiya narrated the story of her neighbors' son in Feel Khana who lost his arm in the belt which rotates the buffing machine in a polishing unit:

Poor thing, he was only twelve years old. The story is that this clothes got caught in the machine. He tried to disentangle them and his hand got caught. Now he's OK. He can even work with one arm.

Khalida said smilingly:

Accidents can happen any time on any job but you can't stop working. The disc of the grinder sometimes breaks and eyes get damaged. The crucible slips and hands and feet get burnt. But if a mother was to think of all these factors, how will she send her child to work?

I asked why most of the children were working in the three or four most hazardous jobs like moulding, polishing,electroplating and welding. Ruksana's answer was:

These jobs have quick returns. A boy who goes to work at a bhatti will get at least Rs 5 at the end of ten hours. This is not the case with skilled jobs like engraving,colouring, etc. For these jobs,you'll notice only those children who are working with their own fathers. The training period is long and there are immediate monetary returns.

It takes a long while before the child can earn enough. As it is, the rate paid to adult engravers is so little that children will get nothing for this. This work is the least harmful. Your clothes don't get spoilt. You don't inhale fumes and dust. The children who used to do a lot of engraving earlier have now virtually disappeared. Many men want these jobs because they are relatively easy, so where is the question of young boys getting them? It is only the very unskilled jobs that children get and unfortunately these are also the most hazardous.

It is clear that the majority of child workers in brass ware industry are engaged in intrinsically hazardous occupations. With the current technology, one does not see any way in which their health can be protected or the health hazards significantly lessened.

EDUCATION

None of the working children I met were educated. They worked a minimum of ten hours a day and their parents said they were not in a position to pay for their education. I talked to Sayeedbhai a painter. His older son was busy colouring a brass plate. He has not been educated. But the younger boy goes to school. He does not want to send his child to work. He said:

You can't sacrifice your family for work. It is bad enough that one son has not been educated and therefore he has to work that this job. But this little one will study. He can always learn the craft. After all, he belongs to a family of artisans. In any case,education will only improve his ability to work.

Others gathered around and said the same thing:'Education is very important if one day you want to become an entrepreneur. To manage the business, the child will have to be given education.

I asked why some parents send their children to work and others do not. And the unanimous responses were:'If you can't feed your children,where is the question of paying for their education? But when I said that primary school education was free for children, they said:

Are there enough schools in Moradabad? Our children don't get admission into government schools and we can't afford to pay Montessori school fees. If there were more schools, half our problems would be solved.

I asked whether parents comes up with a scheme to provide education to all children and sets up schools,all these children working in darja bhattis (box mould furnace) would leave work and go to school. No one sends their children to work because they think that education is irrelevant. But if there are no schools, then children are sent to work.

The attitudes of parents sometimes differed. Zakiabi's husband has deserted her. She lives with her four sons in her sister's house. Although she did not work herself, she sent all her children to work, though they were under twelve years. She said,'Their father has deserted us and gone away so they'll have to work. If he comes back, he can educated them.'

She was so upset about having been deserted that she felt that it was the duty of her children to work and support her. Her young sever-year old son was working in a box mould furnace workshop. He had never been to school. When I asked him how many years he had worked, he said that he did not know how to count but he had been working for several years. The others workers said that he had worked for three years.

In Kathghar,Jamalbhai was working at a box mould furnace workshop with two boys aged eight and ten years. The three together earned Rs 40 a day. The boys were not his sons. He said, 'I have only four daughters so the question does not arise. But if I had a son I would send him to school. This is no work for a child.'But in Peergave, Kathghar, Lal Masjid and Idgah,none of the working children had been to school .

Some parents felt that, 'If they study,they will dies of starvation.' They could not afford the opportunity cost of sending a child to school because every penny earned was crucial for bare survival of the family.

Hafizbhai Namunewala was adamant and said that the problem of child labour was closely linked to the problem of illiteracy. He said, 'I'll give it to you in writing that educated parents do not send their children to work. It is only illiterate parents who put their children to work at an early age.' He went on to add:

It is a vicious circle. If you are uneducated, you don't even understand the implications of what you are doing. You only think of today. It is almost impossible to explain to uneducated people the valued of family planning, for instance. This only makes the problems more difficult to handle. For them, if a child is bringing in one or two rupees at the end of the day, it is good enough.

His son, Mushahid, interjected:'Education is the most important thing. If you are uneducated,you don't even know the meaning of the work bhavishya (future).' Hafizbhai said:

We have had a law to ban child labour for so long. Has it ever been implemented ? Do you know the laws in Japan? You cannot employ a child there. What prevents the government from enforcing the Child Labour Act and forcing parents to educate their children?

I replied that government officials often say that banning child labour is impossible because the economic condition of the families of working children will become worse. Hafizbhai had this to say:

It is true that many families rely entirely on their children. But not always because of economic necessity. In our neighborhood, there are families where the father spends the whole day playing cards. The mother does housework. The only income of that family is from the children. do you think that this should continue? Parents can also be callous. I met a woman this morning who was very upset because her twelve-years old son collapsed in a factory due to heat stroke and she had to spend Rs 30 on doctor's fees and medicines. If parents do not know what is good for their children, then surely the state has to intervene. The consequences of all this are very serious. These are the very children who as adolescent boys become irresponsible citizens. They have so much anger within them. They are the easiest targets for anti-social activity.

Some Muslim social activists confirmed this:

The child who is denied education and made to work is really frustrated. It comes out in little things like his inability to read the film posters. He feels ashamed that he has to ask another child which film is showing. An this alone can build up into a tremendous anger. There is so much violence in our mohallas, in our families-because of this.

Rahim khan,designer,has educated all his children. He said:

The evidence of what education can do for you is all around us. Look at the exporters, they have become multi-millionaires look at us artisans-uneducated-how easily we are being exploited. If you are educated, you know what the laws are, the government policy is. Even if government has a programme for helping the artisans, they don't know about these things. Exporters have got so many concessions and income tax exemptions that overnight they have become multi-millionaires. One of our biggest exporters has recently imported a twelve-seat Toyota from Japan. A car which will cost only Rs 60 on diesel from Moradabad to Delhi. They have four gunmen and guard dogs. Their imported German dog costs them Rs 3000 a month on food and sleeps in an air-conditioned room with one attendant. It is more that what they will spend on ten workers. How have they become so wealthy but by exploiting the uneducated workers?

The people gathered around were very resentful of those who had made it big. Many of them felt that the main road to upward mobility was education. It was the very first step. Without it, the question did not arise. One or two people were of the view that:

The only way to implement a ban on child labour is to use police force. You have to make education compulsory. You provide school books, clothes, etc. Parents will protest. Employers will protest. But sooner or later they will realize that this is all for the good of the child.

Abidbhai said:

It is very important to educate women. If you educate a boy, it is like educating one person. But if you educate a girl she in turn will educate her children. The condition of a family depends a lot on the women. Parents need to be educated on the harmful effect of work on the health of their children.

Hafizbhai added,'Give education to children and their eyes will open up automatically.' Mukhtiarbhai spoke bitterly of the problems of education in Moradabad. He said, 'There is nothing called a school teacher here. In front of my house there is a government school. There are supposed to be four teachers but not one comes. According to him,most of the schools are grant-in-aid schools getting funds from the government and run by registered societies. At the time of school admission and just before examination,they demand money in the form of donations on the slightest pretext. The private schools are not recognized by the government and their certificates and diplomas are of no use for college admissions. Muktiarbhai had a valid point regarding the medium of instruction which is Hindi:

The medium of instruction in Moradabad is Hindi because that is supposed to be our national language. Yet university education in places like Delhi is all in English. Our children are handicapped. And if truly the intention is to use

Hindi,then why is all the literature on the subject or imports and exports in English? All the information we need about government policies and programmes regarding trade are in English. How are we supposes to understand that? Those who are educated in English are obviously at an advantage. Now any body who makes it as an entrepreneur sends his child to Nainital or Dehra Dun for education. Even the better-off artisans are trying to send their children there. But very few can afford it.

Surinder Singh, an activist in Moradabad, but not working with brass workers, had ideas about the kind of education working children need:

I was a child worker myself so I know what it means to be a working child. My father died when I was seven years old and my mother forced me to work.My clothes were always torn and dirty and I was very ashamed of myself. It was only after I had worked for some years, saved some money and bought some clothes that I went to a teacher I knew in the village to let me come to school . Even then, the first day, I was scared. I didn't have the nerve to enter the school, so I stood outside the gate the whole day. It was only when the teacher I knew came that I went with her. Working children have very low self-esteem. They will not even go and talk to a child who is better dressed-because that signifies superior status. The teacher in our society is glorified as the guru close to god- a position that we can never hope to attain. The image must change if children are going to enjoy school. The teacher must come down from her pedestal. Any scheme to provide education to working children must take this into account. Children must be given uniforms so that some semblance of equality can be maintained. If education is to be provided after work, it has to be qualitatively different from that given to non-working children. It must be fun. There must be a component of entertainment in it for it to be successful.

The most horrifying consequences of working in the brass ware industry for children is that their lives are shortened by the hazards they are exposed to. Those who survive are often ill. Their life-chances are bleak because of their illiteracy and the question of bettering their lot simply does not arise; they are thus destined to remain poorly paid and unskilled workers for whatever is left of their lives. Given the nature and kind of for whatever is left of their lives. Given the nature and kind of work, part-time education is not a practicable proposition and it will be impossible to monitor such a scheme. The only solution is to lessen the awesome human cost and pay those parents who cannot afford the money to send their children to school.

TECHNOLOGY AND EMPLOYMENT:SOME OBSERVATIONS

One of the objectives of this study was to see whether any changes in technology could be recommended form the point of view of discouraging the use of child labour and promoting the employment of adults. On a visit to Bangkok in Thailand in 1988, I was able to visit four factories manufacturing brass w are. At each factory there were only eight to ten workers employed but the premises of these factories were almost as large as some of the biggest factories in Moradabad. When I looked at the processes in these factories, it became apparent that the technology used in Bangkok was virtually the same as that used in Moradabad. However, there were no children working in the brass ware factories in Bangkok.

It is relevant to mention here the differences in the technology employed between Bangkok and Moradabad. For one thing, the moulds and crucibles used were of much larger size and could not therefore be handled by children. In one factory for example, where large statues of the Buddha were being made, I saw a crucible being lifted by two men with the aid of wooden supports. Clearly, such heavy weights could not be lifted by children. When I enquired with the factory supervisors as to why children were not employed, they gave three types of reasons. They pointed out that children were not fit by virtue of their physical attributes to work for the industry, that the work was hazardous and therefore not suitable for children and ,finally, that child labour could be obtained in Bangkok only on a monthly wage as most children came from outside Bangkok to work and not on piece-rate wages. In one of the factories I visited where smaller decorative brass pieces were virtually identical to those in Moradabad. Even then, no children were to be seen.

It is not as if there is no child labour in Thailand in general or Bangkok in particular. In fact, Bangkok attracts working children from the poorer Northern and North-Eastern provinces of Thailand. Several studies point out that there are over two million working children in Thailand, a significant proportion of whom are to be found in Bangkok(Bond 1982:2;Udomakdi 1986:36). But perhaps there are better options available for children than working in the brass ware industry and therefore no child works in this industry. It is therefore necessary to look at the relationship between technology and the employment of children in a larger socio-economic setting.

When I spoke to manufacturers and exporters in Moradabad, they informed me that the technology employed in Taiwan and Korea in the brass ware industry was far more sophisticated than that used in Moradabad. The level of mechanization was much higher. In these countries, brass ware is manufactured by the die-casting method where an initial model or die is made and fixed on machines and thousands of pieces are then churned out. Clearly, in more developed capitalist economies, technologies of mass production are more in vogue. Since I have not studied the growth and development of the brass ware industry elsewhere, it is not possible to make further generalizations regarding the situation in those countries.

If one was to posit that increased mechanization in the brass ware industry of Moradabad is a desirable goal from the point of view of discouraging the use of child labour, the first question that needs to be answer is whether there is any incentive for an entrepreneur to take such an investment decision. It was pointed out to me in Moradabad that there have been periods as long as four or five years-such as, for example , after the 1980 riots- when trade saw a sharp decline because there was virtually no production. The regain one's position in the last couple of years that the industry is on the upswing. Apart from other factors like the inherently unstable international market, the uncertain communal situation of Moradabad is a risk to be constantly borne in mind. Such reasons inhibit technological investment and change. Moreover, we have to ask whether it is not cheaper for the entrepreneur to continue at the present technological level when labour in general is cheap and child labour particularly so. The answer, it would appear, in the context of the uncertainties of production and the market, to stick to cheap child labour unless pressure is brought upon the industry through importers.

Let us look at a small technological change that is possible. In the moulding units, there are usually one adult and two or three children. One child is exclusively engaged in rotating the wheel which fans the furnace. In very few units I noticed that a low horsepower motor was installed which routed the wheel and eliminated the need for one child. When I asked other entrepreneurs why this simple device was not more widely used, I was told about-and in fact experienced-the extremely erratic power supply available in the town. since power shortage is a way of life, most people preferred to keep a child worker fanning the furnace for, otherwise the entire production process would grind to a halt whenever why even such small technological changes are not introduced.

In the polishing units, which along with the moulding units are the largest employers of children, the buffs on the polishing machines wear away in course of time. These buffs can be replaced by purchasing them in the market but until it becomes absolutely necessary to replace them, recycled buffs are used for as long as possible. In every polishing unit, one or two children spend most of their time extending the life of these buffs by putting gum, emery powder and some mixture on them. We may infer that the entrepreneur has calculated that it is cheaper for him to employ these children to recycle these buffs rather than buy them from the market. This story illustrates the relatively weak financial position of the entrepreneur who owns a small polishing unit. One cannot expect substantial investment in new technology from persons of such standing, unless those who get this work done also share their profits more equitably. Pressure can again be brought upon these small entrepreneurs only through the industry and that also when there is pressure upon the industry from the buyers of such goods.

I have in the section on the female worker referred to the fact that when there were technological changes in the process of scraping and polishing, women who usually did this work at home were substantially displaced from the labour force. Men took over this job on machines in factories and workshops. As a result, incomes of families in which women did this work saw a decline. To make ends meet in such families, young boys who might otherwise have been in school were sent out to work.

Even if it were feasible to introduce mechanization in the brass ware industry in the background of the hurdles described above, it is necessary to ask whether increased mechanization is a desirable goal considering the prevalence of unemployment and under-employment. Technological changes on a large scale would almost certainly diminish opportunities of employment and under-employment. Technological changes on a large scale would almost certainly diminish opportunities of employment for adults even if such changes made children unsuitable as workers in the brass industry. Perhaps a better alternative would be to bring pressure upon the industry as a whole from the buyers of these goods and entrepreneurs, both big and small are forced to improve working conditions for labour welfare as well as to ensure that no child labour is employed. When there is a continued demand for the goods and non-availability of child labour, it is likely that the prospects of adults workers will improve.

THE IMPLICATIONS OF GOVERNMENT POLICY FOR THE BRASS WARE INDUSTRY

What holds good for the lock, gem,glass and pottery industries is also the case for the brass ware industry of Moradabad-everywhere, child labour is being passed off as family labour, despite facts to the contrary. And this is precisely because of the provision in the Child Labour(Prohibition and Regulation) Act. The fact that work is carries out in residential premises lends credence to the belief that the industry is cottage oriented and that fathers pass on their skills to sons. The labor Department of the Government of Uttar Pradesh organized a sample survey in 1986 and found that only 25 percent of the children were wage workers and that, therefore,protection was required only for 2000 children. My estimates were that there were between 40,000-45,000 children working in the industry, the vast majority of whom are wage workers. the sight of adults males working with children reinforces the view that children work as part of family labour. Patient investigation in needed into these appearances and governmental survey staff are notably untrained for this type of work. When governmental teams visit, they are blandly told on non-existent family connections for people are afraid of violating the law for fear of being penalized. In the short time violating the law for fear of being penalized. In the short time available ,data collectors take what they are offered at face value. It bears repetition that while the work of engraving and colouring is done in family units, at least 75 percent of the child labour force is engaged on work like moulding, electroplating, welding and polishing. These are all extremely hazardous occupations and, if properly investigated, would fall squarely within the purview of the Child Labour Act:

On plank of National Child Labour Programme (NCLP)

is to effectively implement the various laws enacted for the benefit of working children. But the labour office in Moradabad is grossly understaffed with only one labour inspector for the whole city. No organization, however sincere, could even get the facts straight-much less implement the law- when it is so thinly peopled. It is necessary both to sensitize the labour enforcement machinery to the problems of workers-both adults and children-as so as to be able to cover the large area of the industry.

The Government of India has laid down the framework of the NCLP and left it for the local authorities to implement. A bureaucratic tendency to accept what has come form above has led to a plan divorces from reality. The identification of hazardous and non-hazardous activities has been left for the Deputy Director of Factories(Medical) of Uttar Pradesh to decide at a later date. In the meanwhile, it is planned to give vocational training to children in the age-groups often to twelve years and twelve to fourteen years in the trades of engraving polishing, foundry,gas welding,soldering and electroplating. To suggest that children between the ages of ten to twelve years should start with polishing and foundry work would be an express violation of Article 24 of the Indian Constitution. However, given the way in which the Child Labour Act is formulated, if these processes are taught in government-aided schools and institutions, these children would not come under the purview of the law. Thus what may be against the spirits of the Constitution may be perfectly legal!

But it would seem that the proposal under consideration to train twelve to fourteen year old children in soldering electroplating, gas welding, etc.,in factories would also violate Section 67of the Factories Act. The section unequivocally states that children below the age of fourteen years should not be allowed to work in any factory. The scheme for such training. if a approved by the Government of India, was to start in 1988-9 giving stipends and food to the children to be trained in local workshops.

Even if it were not the intention,a scheme to train children in the listed trades will result in providing skilled labour to the brass ware industry at no cost to the industry itself. Had free primary education been offered instead, these children would have had better life chances that their current dismal prospects of remaining workers forever.

Under the NCLP, there is a plan to improve the working conditions in the workshop where children above the age of fourteen years are working. In the areas of child labour concentration, the removal of slums, improvement of sanitation and construction of approach roads are components of the plan in general. For anyone who has visited Moradabad, this scheme appears to be unrealistic for the improvement of working conditions would be close to being impossible unless the entire city is demolished and rebuilt. Obviously, this is not a practicable proposition.

When this case study was written in 1988, a scheme, the Peetal Vasti or colony for brass-workers was being set up outside the city centre by the U.P. States Brass Ware Corporation. This would enable the artisans to move out of this congested living and working quarters to a space allocated outside the city centre. Here, perhaps plots could be allotted only to those families who undertook not to send their children to work but to keep them compulsorily in schools in Peetal Vasti. If the problems that poor children face in schools are taken care of and if an enforcement system devised, then such a scheme might well be viable.

Ultimately, the only solution to the problem of child labour.in the brass ware industry is a complete and unequivocal ban on its use. This step would be in keeping with the stated with the stated policy of the Government of India, which says that it will not allow children to work to hazardous occupations. The National Institute of Occupational Health could do an epidemological study to verify the extent of the problem of health hazards to child workers. The ban would have to be enforced only when the government is ready to provide free, compulsory primary education with the added incentives of free meals, uniforms and books. Exporters, to whom various concessions are given by the government, could be prevailed upon to pay a cess to help fund such a programme.

6

Children in the Glass Industry

Mohit, age sixteen or seventeen years: 'I started working at the age of six earning Rs 5 for a six-hour shift. Today I make Rs 19 a day in a twelve- hour shift blowing glass. A blow glass worker can only work for ten years. Working for twelve to fourteen hours a shift means that the life of a worker is shortened by half. By the time a glass blower has reached thirty years of age, be the time a glass blower has reached thirty years of age, be cannot work much. Soon I will not be able to work as a glass blower. If I manage to save money, I'll start a shop; otherwise, when I have children, I will send them to work.

'We visited Ferozabad in July 1986, to study the glass industry and the conditions of workers there. While the first part deals with the plight of workers in general, the second part addresses itself to child workers in particular. Visits to factories, interviews with factory owners and local government officials and lastly, discussions with some villagers of the area, built up a horrifying picture of the appalling conditions under which children and adults use up their lives in the glass factories of Ferozabad. This experience of twentieth-century India does appear to be significantly different from what industrial workers in nineteenth-century England must have gone through. As we shall see later, some of Marx's observations about the predicament of workers in his time appear to be remarkably apposite

THE ORGANIZATION OF THE GLASS INDUSTRY

Ferozabad is a tehsil (an administrative unit of the district) in Agra district of Uttar Pradesh (U.P)It is also the home of the glass bangle and glassware industry, which is a multi-crore business. Out of 289 registered units (of which 133 units are registered as glass-blowing factories), approximately 70 per cent are not in fact working. However, they get their coal quota at controlled rates and sell it at a 100 per cent premium. The Labour Department certifies that on the day of inspection a particular number of workers were working at a particular unit. The Excise Department gives a certificate of production on the basis of which the Director of Industries recommends a coal quota. On record, even the temperature in the furnace is mentioned t0o prove that the factory was actually working (Chatterji 1986:123; Pal 1986: and Barse 1986a). People say that the owners of bogus units can earn as much as Rs 10 lakhs (Rs 1 lakh is equivalent to Rs 100,000) a year through the black marketing of coal without lifting a finger (Awasthi 1986: 127). Workers cited the example of Som Glass Works where many of them were working. This unit had not functioned for five years but they had been getting a regular coal quota at the controlled rate. Any units which had permanent labourers have shut down their units in order to get rid of their permanent workers. Today, Labourers are recruited on a daily basis in the labour markers at Kotla Mohalla and Ghantaghar. They are, therefore, totally at the mercy of the employers.

The black-marketing of coal allows factory owners to keep their units closed and yet make money. Since 1974, the Uttar Pradesh government has stopped the setting up of new industrial units which use coal as their main source of fuel. Bogus units established earlier can then sell their coal quota at a 100 per cent premium to units which are operating. In this way, they are able to earn money without the burden of running a factory.

Another common practice in Ferozabad is that units close for part of the year, ostensibly for furnace repairs. Workers, however, have a different story to tell, According to them, a taarkash (the man who threads hot glass onto a rolling pin) make 400-500 toras (strings of 312 bangles) in one shift which goes on for at least twelve hours. (Officially, there are supposed to be three, eight-hour shifts). However, for purposes of tax, they show that only 200 toras are made. The profits made on the side allow the factory owners to shut down the factories for part of the year while they live off their illegal profits and their coal quotas (Pal 1986) This is also true of glassware production. Now that there is no excise verification on goods produced, the amount of black money made is even more and the effect on labour is obvious. The sum total of it all is that since factories remain closed for much of the time, Where there should be a shortage of labour, there is in fact a surplus of labour.

Factory owners and government officials deny that there is any exploitation of workers in the glass industry. According to them: 'How can there be exploitation if workers come willingly to work? Yet many factory owners admit that they have dispensed with their permanent staff. According to the proprietor of the Saraswati Glass Works, Till 1965 they had only permanent workers. They were entitled to only three days leave with pay in a year. But in 1980-1, the rules changed and permanent workers were entitled to fourteen days leave with pay.

It was therefore decided to do away with all permanent staff. In 1986, he gave forty workers about Rs 2.75 lakhs and asked them to leave. Talking about the advantages of daily wage workers, he said quite candidly: 'the temporary worker knows he can be removed. It is easier then to get work out of him.

This was amply substantiated by what workers had to say. A Taarkash said:

Everyone says that a Taarkash gets Rs 150 a shift and a belanwala gets Rs 80 for working in one shift. But no one ever asks how many days in a week we get to work. In peak season, a taarkash or a belanwala gets work for three days a week and never for more than four or five months in the year.

A Jagaiya explained his helplessness and pointed out that he could not bring the same man for more than seven days to the factory. If he did so because he felt that the man needed the money, he would be in danger of losing his own job. In the same way, if the factory, owner feels that a particular worker is indulging in netagiri (politicking) or union-baji (unionizing), then the Jagaiya has no choice but to abide by the wishes of the factory owner and not to recruit the man, however unfair the decision might be.

When work is scarce, workers are prepared to work on any terms. As one belanwala pointed out:

I have been unemployed for two weeks, I finally went to the Jagai and told him that I would give a percentage of my wages to him.

It was settled that the Jagaiya would get Rs 80 from the factory but pay him only Rs 65 This apparently is the order of the day.

The local mafia (thugs and goons hired by factory owners) not only prevents labour trouble in Ferozabad but also prevents highly skilled Labourers from moving away from their factories, For example, if a man ha mastered the art of blowing a particular type of fine glass for which the factory owner has got a big order, then it is virtually impossible for that worker to leave. It goes without saying that if the worker leaves, the order is lost, Many big companies like Air India, Oberois, ITDC (India Tourism Development Corporation) and Nestles order their glassware from Ferozabad. It is not unknown for a worker to be killed if he threatens to take business away. Thus while thugs prevent highly skilled workers form taking business away, they also ensure that other workers do not create union trouble and do not insist upon their rights to minimum wages and better conditions of work. In Ferozabad, workers are subject to severe exploitation and their circumstances are akin to those of the labourers of nineteenth-century England. They have on choice but to work twelve to fourteen hours a day, If they refuse, there are always unemployed people waiting to take over their jobs.

DANGEROUS WORKING CONDITIONS

Workers in the glass industry are intimidated for a variety of reasons. One important reason why factory owners need a mafia it to hush up the many industrial accidents that take place because the working conditions are notably unsafe. The industry is technologically very primitive and the pressure on the workers is tremendous. There are two types of furnaces used - the pot furnaces for making only bangles and the tank furnaces which make a variety of glassware as well as bangles. The pot furnace unit is smaller and can run only twelve hours and therefore there is only one shift. The temperature in these furnaces ranges between 700-800 C. The tank furnace units are much bigger and the temperature goes upto 1800 C. In the summer months, the temperature is so high that only the most tenacious workers can manage to work in the excruciating heat. Combined with this heat, in factories where glasses are made in presses, the noise is deafening. The heat, noise and dust obviously have serious ill effects on the health of workers (Chatterji 1986;Barse 1986 b, c). The net effect is that tuberculosis (TB) is widespread and the life of a worker is cut short by ten to fifteen years. But since there is no dearth of labour, to the factory owner it makes no difference what happens to the worker.

Marx pointed out that this was a result of the demands of capitalism which puts a tremendous pressure on the worker and which consequently leads to '..... generations of stunted, short-lived and rapidly replaced human beings, plucked, so to speak, before they were ripe' (Marx [1867] 1982: 380). Writing about the over-worked labourer in 1833, he observed that they 'die off with strange rapidity; but the places of those who perish are instantly filled, and a frequent change of persons makes no alteration in the scene' (ibid.).This is also the case with glass workers in Ferozabad. At a pakai bhatti (a unit where bangles are baked in layers on metal sheets covered with silica sand) in village Chandwar, a worker had fainted due to heat exhaustion, This worker is a pakaiwala (the person who places trays of bangles into the furnace and also stokes it) and is thirty-six years old. The heat in the pakai bhatti is unbearable and it was not possible to stand even ten feet away from the furnace. This man started working at the age of eight and this summer he has fainted three times due to dehydration. He told me that he has only one more month of working life left in him. If he faints once more, he will tell the thekedar (contractor) to find another pakaiwala to replace him. According to this pakaiwala, there is an unwritten rule that a worker, when he is about to collapse, warns the thekedar.

No factory owner wants a labourer to die on the premises as there would be an inquiry and compensation would have to be paid. Workers said that in summer 200-400 glucose drips were given daily to workers who faint with dehydration and heat exhaustion. Private practice is flourishing in Ferozabad where there are almost 200,000 workers employed. Each glucose drip costs Rs 65 Depending on how urgently the work needs to be done and how indispensable the worker is, the factory owner pays for the treatment. Otherwise, the worker borrows from others. The greatest fear of a worker is to collapse with heat exhaustion. He not only loses his day's wages but also has to borrow for expensive treatment (Pal 1986). Factory owners, however, dent that serious industrial accidents take place. The proprietor of one of the biggest glass factories in Ferozabad, in fact said that except for the occasional case of heat exhaustion, workers did not suffer from any adverse effect of intense heat. In his factory, cut nimmbu (lemon) is freely available to workers if they feel the heat very acutely, he proudly added.

A noticeable feature in many factories is that workers in fact display few visible injuries and burn marks. The workers' explanation for this state of affairs is that factory owners do not employ anybody other than a very healthy person. They not only cannot afford to have a death on their premises but the work involved is so strenuous and the conditions so appalling that only the healthiest survive. A mutha uthanewala (the man who removes the spring of hot bangles from the rolling Pin) said that factory owners and the supervisor decide how much a man can make in a day. If a worker produces less than the required quantity, he is dismissed without wages or with only half the wages, Since there are always plenty of desperate people who are unemployed, the Jagai looks around for somebody in very good health.

Glass bangles are being made illegally in tank furnaces since 1982 because the capacity of tank furnaces is greater and they run round the clock. Owners of tank furnaces openly make glass bangles because there is no excise duty on them. These bangles are of slightly inferior quality as the colour is put on them after the molten glass comes out of the tank furnace. These factories also make laboratory equipment, bulbs, chimneys, glassware, etc. Out of sixty glass manufacturing units, only twenty-one units are registered for purposes of excise. From the 1986-7 budget onwards, production verification has stopped. Whatever the factory owners declare as shier production is accepted for purpose of Central excise. In 1985-86, the excise revenue was to the tune of Rs one crore. In

1986-87 the estimated revenue was the supposed to be not more than Rs 15 lakhs. On record the production of glassware has gone down by a third. There is absolutely no control now on what the factory makes and sells. 30 to 40 per cent of the total production of a tank furnace unit is in making bangles where the profit is as high as 50-60 per cent

The story of Ferozabad is one of power, corruption, blackmail and exploitation. The inhuman conditions of work take their toll upon the health of workers. A man by the time he is thirty-five years old is almost finished and has to rely upon his children to save him from starvation and imminent death. There are almost 50,000 children below the age of fourteen years working in the glass industry making it one of the highest concentration of child labour in the world. If a person starts working at the age of eight or nine, he is burnt out by the time he is thirty-five. Poverty and ill-health force him to use his children and the vicious cycle continues inexorably.

In these conditions, what is the future of the workers of Ferozabad? Is there any hope that this vicious cycle will ever be broken? Workers in the glass industry have some suggestions which they feel will go a long way in improving their lives. They want that the Government of India Institute a high-level investigation into the black marketing of coal. If the government was able to stop the coal allotment to bogus units which have closed down on the pretext of seasonal repairs, it would force factory owners currently living off black money to reactivate their factories. If all the registered units were actually working, there would not be able to exploit the workers so easily. If there is full employment, the economic condition of workers will automatically improve.

PLIGHT OF CHILD WORKER

The plight of child workers is indeed painful. As mentioned earlier, the two boys working in the glass industry were both left behind by their parents to pay off loans. They were lonely, homesick and had to live by themselves at the pakai bhatti, cook their food on silica covered trays and work near furnaces whose temperatures went up to 800 c. The older boy was studying in school till a few a few months back, when his father had an accident working on a thresher and lost his arm and the boy was withdrawn from school and brought to Ferozabad. His father had taken an advance from the thekedar and the boy was to pay off the loan from his wages.

The other boy comes from Tundla village in Agra district; His father also took an advance of Rs 500 from the thekedar and left his little boy behind. On being asked whether he had any brothers and sisters, the boy put his head down and began to cry. An old man sitting next to him explained that the boy was feeling homesick as his father had just come a few days previously to collect his wages and had gone back to the village without him.

Interviews with workers, factory owners and the local MLA revealed that there are almost 50,000 children below the age of fourteen year working in the glass industry at Ferozabad: the total labour force is estimated at 200,000.

A visit to any glass unit shows at a glance that at least 25 per cent of the workers present are children. The official figures reported by the Labour Department estimate that there are 65,000-70.000 workers and that children constitute only 13 per cent of the total labour force. Official figures are considerably lower than what was reported in the field. Ferozabad would then appear to have one of the largest concentrations of child labour in India.

PARTICIPATION OF CHILDREN IN THE WORK FORCE

Child labour is a touchy issue in the glass industry because of government's recent interest in the subject. In fact, according to factory owners and government officials, children are employed only to serve water to adult workers. But when faced with the facts, they present a complete volte-face and plead the case for the poor thus:

What can we do when fathers bring their children to us and beg us to employ them?If we did not help out, these poor people would starve.

While factory owners make out that they are in fact helping the poor to survive by employing their children, the arithmetic of glass manufacture tells a different tale. Child labour is so important for the glass industry that if factory owners did not employ children, their production would go down by 25 per cent. The owner of a big glass factory went to the extent of saying that 'the glass industry cannot function without children. They run much faster than adults and therefore production goes up.

Children perform a variety of jobs in the glass industry. Their work is not very different from that of children in nineteenth century England. A tour of four of the largest glass-blowing units and one glass bangle unit (where only bangles are made) showed that children are involved in almost all the processes of bangle-making and glass-blowing and many of these processes are extremely hazardous for them.

Ashok, an eleven year-old glass factory worker, was interviewed by film maker meera Dewan. He describes his first day at work when he did three shifts. He was new to the job and therefore made a small mistake and was beaten up for it.

I was so tired, I didn't do the work correctly, I made a mistake. This man next to me, he gave me a slap.... it was such a hard slap that I couldn't ever forget the work now.(target 1996:54).

Children do all manner of jobs in glass factories. They were seen carrying molten glass on a seven-foot iron rod called labya from the furnace to the adult worker and back to the furnace. Nearly 85 per cent of the total child labour force was engaged in the this activity and these are Labour Department figures.

Children sit in front of furnaces where the temperature

is said to be about 700 c. In many of the factories where the children were drawing molten glass from tank furnaces in which the temperature was between 1500 c and 1800 c, the face of the child was within six to eight inches from the opening of the furnace. Since he was small in size, he had to put his arm right inside in order to draw adequate quantities of molten glass. As a result, his body was almost touching the furnace.

Most visitors to Ferozabad are taken on a conducted tour of some so-called model factories such a Advance Glass Works and Om Glass Works, who are makers of high-quality glassware for companies such as Air India. In these factories, child labour exists as well but one does not notice children so much because they are relatively spacious; after the factory owners have told the visitor their human interest stories of poverty and child labour, one can actually leave the factory premises believing that factory owners are in fact doing the poor a good turn by employing their children. If however, one manages to visit factories other than the ones highly recommended, the conditions are well and truly horrifying.

One such factory is the General Traders (GT) Glass Works where the bulk of the glassware is made in automatic presses. Like other factories, they also make bangles and blow glassware. It is frightening to enter this factory where obviously labour inspections. have never taken place. The whole factory floor was strewn with broken glass and naked electric wires were to be seen everywhere. The noise in the factory was deafening and there was hardly any space to move without bumping into somebody or other. At least 30-40 per cent of the labour force in this factory seemed to be made up of children of the ages of eight of thirteen years (Barse 1986 a, b, c). They were carrying glasses made in presses on forks to the conveyor belt. They were sitting in front of small furnaces re-heating the loam (molten glass) on which colour had been applied. But mainly, they were engaged in carrying loam on labyas (the seven-foot iron rod used for carrying molten glass). There were children sitting on the ground in front of blow glass workers, closing the mould after the molten glass was put into it. Their job seemed to be to line the mould with paper and close it after the blow glass worker had put the blown glass into it. As soon as the child closed the mould, even before he had time to remove his hands, the mould would catch fire because of the paper inside it. The whole process takes a few seconds from the time the worker brings the molten glass on a labya to the glass blower and the blown glass is put into the mould. After that, children carry the product to another worker who cuts it and then it is taken away for further heating. While I was watching the children at work, about ten to fifteen young workers, including several children ran past me in a passage about three feet wide carrying molten glass. One worker bumped into another and part of the molten glass from his labya fell on inch away from my foot . There was on place to move because behind me were some loose wires and across this narrow passage, other children were sitting on the ground with their backs to the passage in front of small furnaces, re-heating the loam If the molten glass (the temperature of which I was told was nearly 1200 C) had not fallen near my foot, it would have fallen on a child's back. Under these working conditions, it is not surprising that industrial accidents are frequent though government officials and factory owners dent it. People even went to the extent of saying that fatal and near-fatal accident victims are thrown in to the furnaces to destroy evidence (Barse 1986 a.b,c).

Children are undoubtedly the most common victims of such industrial accidents because their bodies cannot take the trauma of such accidents easily. The interesting thing was that in spite of frequent burn injuries and accidents, I did not see any obviously injured worker in the factories. The reason for this was clear after a visit to neighboring villages and conversations with workers.

Sriram, about nine years old, and a thandibatiwala (the person who carries the molten glass after it is beaten into shape, back to the furnace) could not open his left eye which was very sore. A piece of hot glass flew into his eyes. He was being looked after by co-workers as his parents had left him there.

Grace, aged sixteen years, was wounded when he took the spring of glass bangles to show the supervisors. The man tried to break a piece by hitting it. Part of this flew into Graces's face and when I interviewed him, his face looked as if a hive of bees had attacked him.

While workers, including child workers, are paid on a time rate basis in the bigger factories, in the smaller units where bangles are joined in a process called judai (to join),. all workers are paid on a piece-rate basis. In most of these units, particularly the katai addas (unregistered units where designs are cut 0n bangles), children can be seen everywhere. The bangles are brought by the thekedar who has a unit in or near his house. He engages the labour and pays them according to the intricacy of the design. Breakage of bangles while cutting the design is adjusted against the wages of the workers. As it happens, children often end up by losing a whole day' earnings for starts earning a reasonable wage.

The judai addas (unregistered small units where bangles are joined over acetylene flames), also have a very large number of child workers. At one adda (unregistered workshop),out of twenty workers, at least three or four were very small children who were not quite eight. The room was so dark that only their eyes could be seen staring out of the inky blackness. It was lunch-time and the acetylene lamps had been switched off. The room was full of soot and there was no ventilation as the acetylene flames could be extinguished by the breeze. The workers in this unit came from Hallapur village, which is about four kilometers from Ferozabad town, on bicycles. The workers said that 50-60 per cent of this work was done by children and this led to tremendous eye-strain as the worker sat in front of the flames working continuously for twelve hours without removing his eyes from the flame. Many workers said that the high incidence of tuberculosis (T.B.) amongst judai workers was a result of inhaling kerosene fumes (Pal 1986; Champakalakshmi n.d:12).

MINIMUM WAGES

Surprisingly, there are no minimum wages fixed for the glass bangle workers. Minimum wages were first introduced in 1974 for glass bangle and blow glass workers. In 1981, a revision of wages took place by a government order. In 1982, a high powered tripartite committee met and another government order was issued for revision of wages only for the bangle industry. The tripartite committee of labour leaders, union members, employers and government officials fixed the minimum wages and a government order (GO No. 4560(ST)0/36-1-637/ST/81 Lucknow dated November 12, 1982) was passed.

However, after the 1981 government order, the Glass Industrial Syndicate, Ferozabad, filed a writ petition in the Allahabad High court against minimum wages for bangle workers. It is said that the High Court slapped a contempt of court order on the UP Labour Secretary for insisting upon minimum wages for glass bangle workers, The state government withdrew the GO of 1982 by GO No. 4195-36-3-55, dated 25-11-1983.

THE LABOUR DEPARTMENT AND ITS VIEWS ON CHILD LABOUR

Child labour is an indispensable part of the glass bangle and glass-blowing industry of Ferozabad because it is cheap (Chatterji 1986:10;Barse 1986 a,b,c,).The Labour Department at Ferozabad had recommended to the higher authorities that child labour should not be banned because unless a child starts working at a very young age, he will not get acclimatized to the intense heat. They have even suggested that hostels be constructed where children who have to work on the night shift can stay. The argument is that children, who have to work back to the village at that hour and therefore they must have a place to stay. Since the glass industry cannot function without children and they have to run at night because otherwise factory owners will face losses through the heat in the furnaces going waste, children must work at night.

Night-work for children is forbidden under the Factories Act (63 of 1984) which, under Section 70, prohibits the employment even of adolescents below the age of seventeen years. But night-work in the night shift. Factory owners today are not as honest as their counterparts in England in the nineteenth century who admitted that:

Great difficulty would be caused by preventing boys under eighteen form working at night. The chief would be the increase of cost from employing men instead of boys (Marx [1867] 1982: 372)

In fact, this is the main reason why children are employed in the glass industry. Marx sarcastically explains the rationale for exploiting children by factory owners. He said that factory owners were not interested in discontinuing night-work because in industries which use furnaces, not only is there a loss form machinery lying idle but there would be a waste of fuel as well. The argument in favour of night-work was also that otherwise, time would be lost in heating up the furnaces and the furnaces themselves would suffer from changes in temperature.

CHILD LABOUR BUT ADULT UNEMPLOYMENT

In India today, child labour is being justified on the grounds of poverty. If the children of the poor do not work they will starve, it is argued. Another common argument is that will become vagabonds and anti-social elements. These young persons need to be harnessed for productive work. But a fact that is not being recognized is that child labour cannot be justified in a country where there is rampant adult unemployment and under-employment. Ashok (referred to earlier) has an unemployed father. This man told Meera Dewan that he gets up at 4 a.m. to make morning tea for Ashok so that the boy can go to work. He feels bad about making his son go to work, so he helps out in his small way be making the morning tea and bringing Ashok's lunch to the factory (Target 1986:53).

Ashok describes his working day thus:

I pass on the iron rods with the melted glass on it to the blower, come back for a bite, and then go and give the next one (ibid.).

Marx's explanation for why glass manufacturers do not give regular meal-times to children is that it would be time lost or 'wasted' (Marx [1867] 1982: 374). Describing the lives of child labourers in the glass industry in England in 1965, he remarks:

A certain amount of heat beyond what is usual at present might also be going to waste, if meal-times were secured in these cases, but it seems likely not equal in money-value to the waste of animal power now going on in glass-houses throughout the kingdom growing boys not having enough quiet time to eat their meals at ease, with a little rest afterwards for digestion (ibid).

The exploitation of children in the glass industry is to be seen to be believed. Ashok's story is the story of every other boy in Ferozabad, some of them even younger than Ashok.

....I leave the house at four in the morning, after having some breakfast. Then it takes an hour to reach the factory site. I go from one to another, to find out where they need a person to carry the hot iron rods. Sometime, I sit in one factory waiting for the work. If I get it, that's fine. If not I have to go home without the work and money (Target 1986:53-4)-

Child labour is to be found everywhere in the glass factories and although children are engaged in the most dangerous of jobs described earlier, the Labour Department of the State Government in their recent report said that:

Compared to national standards, the above rates per thousand worker population are not alarming. Glass work is known to be less dangerous as compared to chemical works, power generation and basic metal industry (GOUP 1986 a: 6).

The Labour Department Committee was headed by the Deputy Labour Commissioner, Agra and the Assistant Director of Factories (Medical). The Committee, during the course of its inspection, found that:

Children as young as ten years of age were working but the processes in which they were engaged did not call for excessive strength or activity.

Labour laws are openly flouted in Ferozabad with the complete connivance of the local bureaucracy. The Labour Committee Report of April, 1986, Admits that while children under the age of fourteen years are prohibited from working under the Factories Act, yet they found that all the glass-blowing and glass bangle-making factories were employing children. Knowing that this was the case, when 125 factory inspections had taken place up to April 1986, only twelve employers had been prosecuted for violation of Section 67 of the Factories Act, which says that 'no child who has not completed his fourteenth year shall be required or allowed to work in any factory'.

Owners of glass factories are aware that children cannot be employed under the Factories Act. This is why when government teams come to inspect factories, children just disappear. This is what happened when the Labour Department Committee went on its inspection tours. According to its report, Shankar Novelties Glass Industries had violated Section 67; Emkay Glass Works had only four children working because most of the children were removed from the premises as soon as the management came to know about the visit of the Committee in a neighboring factory. This was also the case with the Om Glass Works from where most of the children had been removed before the Committee visited the factory. In the Refugee Glass Works and in Ashok Glass Works, illegal child labour was found.

When every single glass factory in Ferozabad employs children illegally, it is quite obvious from the figures given by the Committee on the number of prosecutions launched under Section 67 of the Factories Act that they have only touched the tip of the iceberg. Instead of condemning child labour and prosecuting employers of child labour, the Labour Department justifies child labour on the grounds that:

* Child labour exists because of poverty.

* The children of the poor are not interested in conventional education.

* This is a hereditary occupation.

* Children need to work at an early age to get acclimatized to the intense heat.

* Most of the work that children do is non-hazardous.

It is undoubtedly true that the children in the glass factories of Ferozabad - like children elsewhere in India - work because their families are poor. But the argument that child labour is therefore necessary must be rejected. To blandly blame the abstract notion of poverty is to ignore the particular economic and social circumstances that contribute not the persistence of child labour. Once these circumstances are analyzed and understood, the possibility of changing them now arises rather than wait for that distant day when there is no more poverty. It is here that the exploitation of the worker by the glass factories of Ferozabad must be viewed as a means of ensuring the privileged position of factory owners. The obnoxious conditions of work shorten the productive life of the worker forcing him then to depend upon the labour of his children. During his productive period, since he gets employment for only a few days in a week and for not more than four or five months in the year, he cannot afford to educate his children; his children, then, are denied the option of breaking away form the rigours of their lives. For small sums of money, parents pledge their children to life-times of bondage. The area MLA and others contended that 90 per cent of the children are bonded slaves.

In the absence of alternative employment opportunities, the workers are dependent for their livelihood on the glass manufacturers. With low and uncertain wages, it is difficult for them to feed their children; the option of sending their children to school is simply not real (Burra 1986 b,c). Not surprisingly, illiteracy is widespread amongst these children. Nevertheless, there are a few examples of parents who have put their desperate economic straits. Said a worker in response to a question as to whether he would train his child in his avocation:

> My life is virtually over at thirty-six. Do you think I want my son to suffer like this? If I can somehow see him through school, I'll try and keep him out of this industry. I don't want my son to die at the age of forty years which is bound to happen to someone working twelve to fourteen hours a day in this intense heat. But I know that I cannot work beyond another month; then how will I pay for his school clothes? If he doesn't have proper clothes, the teacher will not let him enter the class-room. Sooner or later, circumstances will force me to put him to work.

To justify child labour on the grounds that the children need to be acclimatized to the intense heat is only a reflection of our inhuman society which can even make such a suggestion. It has perhaps not even occurred to the Labour Department that such intense heat can in fact have very adverse effects upon the health of the child. Or does the department believe that with growing numbers, the children of the poor are an expendable commodity? And if this is the attitude of the bureaucracy to the plight of working children, then obviously for them the work that children do is in fact non-hazardous.

The premise of the Child Labour (Prohibition and Regulation) Act, 1986, is that there can be no doing away with child labour as it is a consequence of poverty. Such an attitude does not bode well either for the families who are poor or their children who labour. Both Article 24 of the Constitution and Section 67 of the Factories Act explicitly direct that children below the age of fourteen years are not to work in factories. Article 24 forbids the employment of children in hazardous occupations. Yet the Act does not make the glass industry out-of-bounds for children.

The Ministry of Labour has set up a Child Labour Technical Advisory Committee to draw a line between hazardous and non-hazardous processes in hazardous industries: children will be banned from working in the former and allowed to work in the latter. Any attempt to carve out an area of non-hazardous children. This writer believes there can be no non-hazardous process in a hazardous industry. To illustrate, children in the glass factories are always exposed to hot, flying pieces of glass, whatever particular activity they are engaged in. Also, once children are allowed to work in a hazardous industry, who is to police the factory and ensure that they are doing only safe jobs? The answer cannot be a bureaucracy that is corrupt and amenable to power and influence; even assuming it to be conscientious, which bureaucracy can monitor what 50,000 children in the glass industry are doing? More fundamentally, the Committee will not even be able to find children when it visits such factories for they are whisked away whenever an inspection team is around.

What is the future of the children of Ferozabad? They do not have much of a past, steeped as they are in poverty, malnutrition and illiteracy. Their future depends in large part, on governmental response. Today, the prospects for these children are not at all bright. They can look forward to lives very similar to that of their parents, trapped in a web not of their own making. Can we not implement the Constitution of India and provide conditions for universal primary education? Why should the State be so chary and coy in dealing with the vested interests of Ferozabad?

7

Child Labour in the Lock Industry of Aligarh

The patients were all workers in the lock industry employed in paint workshops, polishing or electroplating units. They complained of continuous coughs, blood in their sputum and a feeling that their heads were about to burst. The compounder was making up packets of multi-vitamin tablets.

The doctor was very matter of fact when I asked him why be was prescribing only multi-vitamins when the complaints seemed so serious. His reply was: 'Most of these people are already to for gone. You can't do anything to save them. At least this medicine gives them a feeling that they are being treated. The multi-vitamin capsule looks like a strong medicine. It makes them feel good, when they reach the last stages, I give them cortisone. But death is only a matter of time.

'How can you be so callous?' I asked.

He replied, 'It's not can you tell a lock-maker to stop working if he wants to live? That is his whole life. There are no other opportunities in Aligarh. The entire population is dependent on lock making.

ALIGARH CITY:THE BACKGROUND

Aligarh city is divided into two cleãr-cut halves by a railway line, Which divides the city north/south. In the northern part

There are between 80,000-90,000 workers involved either directly or indirectly in the lick industry. Of the total workers, approximately 7000-10,000 are children below the age of fourteen years. However, these are factory owners and government officials, there are only 5000 children working out of 55,000 workers, comprising 9 per cent of the total labour force. The actual numbers are, however, much larger (Burra 1987a)

Field-work

During field-work I visited about fifty polishing units, fifty electroplating units, twenty painting units as well as thirty homes where either filing or assembling or packing was being done. I was able to visit ten factories in the industrial area and meet scores of workers who were working at home in the city and in the outlying villages. The villages I went to were Bhambola, Jaffarabad and Barola in Aligarh tehsil: however, these visits were not very useful as children were not engaged in hazardous work there. I also visited the inner city a couple of times between 8 p.m. and 11.30 p.m. to see whether children were working at night. I spent twenty-one days in the field on three separate occasions out of the project period of three months.

The Research Assistant, who was employed for a month, had two helpers. to assist him. He was assigned the job of listing the number of units and assessing the number of child, adolescent and adult workers in each unit in thirty mohallas (localities)of the Upper Kote area, which boasts the highest concentration of the most hazardous processes in the lock industry. He went only to those units that were visible from the street but did not attempt to interview the employers of employees both for lack of time and because he did not want to arouse suspicion. In these thirty mohallas, he saw 683 units where the processes of electroplating,spray painting and polishing were being carried out. Apart from these processes, he also observed that the jobs of operating hand-presses, assembling and making keys were being performed in many of these units.

According to the information collected by the Research Assistant. out of 6936 workers in the 683 units visited, there were 2475 children below the age of fourteen years, accounting for 35.68 per cent of the total work force in the sample. Children accounted for more than 50 per cent of all workers only in two areas, Qazi Para and Tan Tan Para., out of the thirty mohallas studied, The data collected indicated the size of the problem even though formal sampling techniques were not employed of the city is the Civil Lines and in the southern portion, the old city. These two portions of the city display a striking contrast where the over spill from the old city, population growth and urban development have resulted in the formation of two distinct cultures and patterns of settlement.

The old city is the ecological centre of Aligarh. This has the tightly knit core of the central business district and fans out towards the eastern-southern suburbs. Most of the Muslim majority mohallas (residential localities). which house both businesses and homes, are located in the centre and are surrounded by Hindu localities. This area is communally sensitive because the residential areas are populated by Muslims but trading and commercial activities are in the hands of the Hindus. It is in centre of Upper Kote, that several small and medium-scale lock-making household industries are located. There is almost on contact between the two areas of the city, the civil lines and the old city.

According to a study on communal violence and its impact on development and national integration conducted by the Centre for Research in Rural and Industrial Development (CRRID) , in Aligarh district of about 1575 registered manufacturing units, it was found that only 7 per cent of the manufacturers were Muslims. And of these 7 per cent, about a fourth of them were involved in the lock-making industry (CRRII n.d.:28) Thus, a very large proportion of industries and manufacturing units in Aligarh are owned by Hindus.

This study also made the significant point that Muslim majority mohallas have fewer educational facilities and the drop-out rate and non-attendance rate of Muslim children were much higher than those of children belonging to other religious, communities. Around 80 per cent of the muslim school children either drop-out or fall in the category of non-attendance'.

Most of the traditional lock-makers-both Hindu and Muslim-are engaged in this work for part of the year as agriculture alone cannot support them. Since most producers are dependent upon others for supply of components, there is a great deal of inter-dependence amongst the castes/communities as certain processes are the exclusive or near-exclusive preserve of certain castes/communities. Thus, The Kohlis (a Scheduled Caste community) are mainly involved in casting activities. Muslims are more of less exclusively doing polishing work and in the final products is done by Muslim Safis, Mathur Brahmins and Jatavs. The suppliers are mainly Hindu Banias (Varshneys). The relationship between the traders and the direct producer of locks is that of super ordination and subordination (CRRID:47). With the coming in of merchant capital, the position of the direct producer has been worsened. His working day has been lengthened and his earning power reduced substantially (ibid.). With the influx of outside capital into the lock industry, there have been structural changes in the industry which have brought about a shift from the household to the factory system, especially in the mode of producing locks

The big lock industry, owned by Hindus, is located in the outskirts of the city, while the smaller units, owned by Muslims, are in the interior. While most of the manufacturing units are owned by Hindus, the labourers are either Muslims or Scheduled Castes leading to tension between them for scarce jobs.

THE LOCK INDUSTRY: A HISTORICAL BACKGROUND

The lock industry of Aligarh was started in 1860 by the Postal Department. In the early years, the making of locks was a village industry and locks or components of locks were made by the artisan in this home, with the help of his family labour. Many families, who found it difficult to support themselves only by agriculture, started making locks. There were also many castes like the maithile Brahmins and others, whose lands were usurped by the Thakurs and big landlords of the area, who then also joined the lock industry. Most of the padlocks were made in the surrounding villages. As the demand for locks increased, the lock-makers found it difficult to commute and many families sold their lands and shifted to the city. But these were essentially small village craftsmen.

After the Partition of India in 1947, there was a sudden shift in the social composition of lock-makers. Many of the traditional lock-makers in Aligarh city were Muslims who when away to Pakistan leaving a void. They were the real real craftsmen and for a while there was slump in the lock industry. While Muslim artisans or master-craftsmen who were the backbone of the lock-industry went to Pakistan, there was a migration of Punjabi Hindus to Aligarh. These families were not engaged in lock making traditionally. But realizing that the lock industry was a profitable venture, they set up small units by hiring labour and this led to the mass production of locks.

Thus, whereas the village craftsman or lock-maker was able to provide for the needs of fewer people, once the indus-trialist stepped in, locks began to be manufactured on the factory scale by people whose main contribution was their capital. The demand for locks has increased tremendously and the lock industry is seen as one with a very good future.

Thus, whereas the village craftsman or lock-maker was able to provide for the needs of fewer people, once the indus-trialist stepped in, locks began to be manufactured on the factory scale by people whose main contribution was their capital. The demand for locks has increased tremendously and the lock industry is seen as one with a very good future.

But inspite of mass-production of locks in factories, the village craftsman has not been wholly displaced. Locks are still being made in the adjoining villages of Pilakhana, Atrauli and Barola. The village artisan brings a model to the financier of well-known lock trader, gets his order, buys the raw material and components, finishes the product and gives it to the trader who then puts a brand name on it such as Parker, Plaza and so on. But the bulk production of locks is locks is done by financiers and lock manufacturers in the big factories.

THE LOCK INDUSTRY TODAY

According to A.L. Anand, in 1982 there were about 3000 units both in the organized and the unorganized sector, manufacturing, assembling locks and their components. There were only five or six units in the large sector; the rest were in the small scale sector. Out of the total units in the small-scale sector, about 150 units were registered and the remaining units were run by artisans as household and cottage industry (Anand 1982Locks or parts of locks are made in almost every home in the old city. The practice of using children as part of family labour is very common. It is estimated that about 80 per cent of the country's locks are made in Aligarh district.

PROCESSES IN THE LOCK INDUSTRY

There are two methods of making padlocks. One is the

traditional method where the lock-maker designs a lock and gets an order from the trader. The trader is usually also a financier who may give a loan to the lock-maker to buy raw material and other components. Once an order is placed, the lock-maker gives the raw material, namely brass or iron, to the dhalai (moulder, who usually belongs to a Scheduled Caste community) along with a model. The dhalai casts all the pieces according to specifications and returns them to the lock-maker who then files them. Those components like the handle, springs, keys, etc., which have not been cast by the dhalai are bought from the market, the lock assembled and then returned to the trader. The trader gets a final polish given to the locks and his brand name engraved on them and then markets them.

Most of the heavy brass and iron locks are made this way. The smaller and less expensive locks with names such as Link, Horseman and Mobaj as well as well as mortice and cycle locks are mass produced in factories. In this process, the lock manufacturers have their own production units where they cut scrap iron sheets called MSA sheets-which they get from the automobile industry-on power presses. Thus the outer cover of locks, the lid, flat keys and other parts are all cut from MSA sheets. Some parts of the lock like the handle are also cut and bent and grooves made in the big factories. Once this is done on power-presses, the work shifts to the hand-presses where the components are smoothened and holes pierced in keys or key-holes pierced in lock-cases. Hand-presses and power-presses are used for a variety of jobs. A die is fitted into the machine which will do a particular job. For every process, there is a separate die.

These rusted components of locks are either sent for dhol (drum)-this is a term used for drum polishing-or polishing on buffing machines. Those parts of a lock which are visible from outside such as the handle, cover or keys, which need to be electroplated, are first polished on buffing machines. Those parts which are not visible are sent for dhol. If visible parts are not electroplated, then they are spray painted.

Children do no work with dhalais, or in dhol polishing, dhol plating or on power-presses. But children are used in all other processes like working on hand-presses, polishing on buffing machines, in electroplating and spray painting units, for filing machines, in electroplating and spray painting units, for filing components, making springs and assembling and packing of locks.

It is important to note here that some of these processes like working on hand-presses, electroplating, buff polishing and spray painting are also done for the hardware industry in Aligarh. Children working in these units are therefore not exclusively working for the lock industry.

There is not even one factory where all the processes (of which there are approximately forty-five are carried out in the same premises. Most of the factories get some parts made outside. The work is given on a contract basis and it is the responsibility of the contractor to get the work done. All workers are paid on a piece-rate basis and work anything upto forty-eight hours at a stretch when the work-load is heavy.

In the big factories, components are cut and then farmed out to artisans to do the filing, finishing, etc. There are different contractors for different jobs and varying systems for getting the work down, Some people are paid by the gross, others are given a weekly wage and still others are remunerated according to lots. Ninety-five per cent of the workers have no protection as they are piece-rate workers.

In some units, popularly known as karkhanas (literally means factory and legally they would come under the Factories Act. 1984 the premises and machines may belong to a man who directly hires labour and gets work done on a lot basis. In yet others, the man who owns the machines may rent them out to different sub-contractors who arrange for the labour, Sometimes a sub-contractor may himself work on the machines, but this is rare. By and large, those who own these machines do not work on them.

In the lock industry the 'putting-out' system prevails for a variety of reasons. Small firms are able to survive because they act as sub-contractors to the larger firms and supply special components and help out at certain stages of production during periods of peak demand. Secondly, legislation such as the Factories Act and various Labour Acts help perpetuate the 'putting out' system, which is the best way of maintaining profits without any obligations to the workers. A third major reason which allows the 'putting-out' system to flourish is that there exists a large number of small peasants in the countryside around Aligarh city. whose lands do not provide a full livelihood; through the 'putting-out' system, they are able to save and then invest the capital in the financing of cottage industry rather than in the factory system.

The small entrepreneur is himself fairly poor and he survives primarily by exploiting those who are even poorer. The small entrepreneur is almost as uncertain about getting work as the labourer and therefore there is a high mortality rate with smaller units having to close down because of economic insecurity.

WAGE STRUCTURE

There is no uniform wage structure in the lock industry. The method of payment is, by and large, the piece-rate system. In one assembling unit, the owner said he paid children Rs 25 a month for a ten-hour day Workers in a polishing unit said that children, if they work twelve to fifteen hours, can earn up to Rs 15 a day and an adult Rs 25 In electroplating units, child workers can earn Rs 5 to Rs 10 a day depending upon the number of hours of work. Many children interviewed said they worked for more than twenty hours at a stretch. They would take a short nap or drink tea if they were very sleepy and continue to work. I met two children who had worked thirty-six hours at a stretch and who were paid 60 paise an hour as over-time Many children, I was told, worked for several months without wages, particularly in the polishing units. After that, they earned Rs 50 a month. Only after working ten to fifteen years was a man able to earn Rs 600 a month and that also for a fourteen - hour day

The payment of low wages to workers have other ramifications as well. Poor parents are not able to afford the expenses of school-going children if the education is not subsidized. But more importantly, as pointed out earlier: 'The generally prevailing low wages/remuneration for work of the parents forces them to involve child labour in the traditional business of the family'.

There is no fixed wage rate and different jobs/processes are paid according to different rates. For example, for cutting a keyhole with a pointed chisel in the lock-case called dibbi (a term used to describe a flat and small box) and also fitting a key, a child earns Rs 3 per thousand and he can complete 1000-1500 holes in a whole working day Sometimes, a child is paid 30-35 paise per gross. Likewise, in a electroplating unit, in an eight to ten hour working day a child could tie 1000-1500 locks/handles on copper wires. For this work, he is paid Rs 2 or Rs 3 per thousand The rate was also fixed at 30 paise per gross.

While there is no uniform wage structure in the lock industry, my interviews revealed that on the average, a child earned nothing for the initial period of apprenticeship, after which he began to earn Rs 50 per month. This unpaid period for learning the skills varied from process to process but rarely exceeded one year. For the first couple of years, the child earned a monthly wage of Rs 50 a month but his working day normally lasted twelve to fourteen hours. He was paid no overtime. On the days that the unit was closed, he got no wages. All units are closed on Wednesdays and units owned by Muslims are also closed on Friday.

After a few years, the child earned between Rs 125-150 per month for a nine-hour working day. He was also paid over-time depending on the urgency of the order and the mood of the contractor. These workers were considered permanent by thekedars (contractors) because they were regular employees but they were not entitled to any other benefits such as medical assistance, Provident Fund and so on. The salaries of these children were also cut for days they were absent due to ill-health or on Wednesdays, when units were closed.

Thus, a child earned Rs 50 a month or about Rs 1.60 paise per day for an average of a twelve-hour day Any day he did 125 a month for a nine-hour day got approximately Rs 4 per day and was not paid for the days he was absent or the factory was closed.

Many explanations were advanced for preferring the piece rate system to a fixed-rate system. According to factory owners, the labourers employed in polishing, electroplating and painting units were prone to alcoholism: if workers were paid fixed wages, they would disappear for days at a time and not come to work. Another unit owner said that this system of payment was best for both labour and factory owners because the factory owner has assured output and the labourer, if he is hard-working and sincere, can earn a lot of money

But the main reason, as another factory owner frankly pointed out, is that polishing, electroplating and spray painting are the three most hazardous processes in the lock industry and h felt that contract labour was not convert by any labour laws. The unit owner has no responsibility to the worker if he falls ill or gets seriously hurt when working and he does not have to provide medical assistance or compensation if the worker dies. This is the primary reason for getting work done on a put-out' system, where the wages are paid according to output and there is no job security.

Workers were interviewed randomly from the neighboring areas, Most of the workers and unit owners were engaged in electroplating, polishing on buffing machines and spray painting. Most of the workers engaged in polishing work live near Mehtab Ka Nakla near Shahja Marg. In this locality, almost 500 children go every day to work in the polishing units in the Upper Kote region. I interviewed six children and seven adults who had been working on buffing machines. They were covered in black emery powder. Although they had bathed after returning from work, the colour of their skin was black. I was told that children, when they start learning this work, do not get any money except for the occasional rupee or two to go to the cinema.

They worked twelve to fourteen hours and were paid monthly wages. The children were between the ages of seven and eleven years. One boy had come home at 2 a.m. when the work was over. He was eleven and had been working for three years. In the first year, he got paid nothing because he was learning the job. In the second year, he received Rs 50 a month. Now, he earns Rs 150 a month. His father is a rickshaw-puller and he has three unmarried sisters. He was never sent to school. He then went to work with another polisher. In the unit where he works now, there are almost twenty workers of whom fifteen are children of his age.

An old man pointed to two small children who were his grandchildren. They were both working as polishers. When I told him that thekedars said they paid children Rs 500 a month, the crowd of about fifteen adults and eight children laughed and said that the children were not even paid Rs 50 And if a person got ill, as was inevitable, he not only lost his day's wages, but also had to borrow money for treatment. On the weekly day off when the power supply was shut off, the worker loses the day's wages.

After working for six months, they start earning Rs 50-60 a month. A child starts working at the age of six or seven years. He usually goes to work along with his neighbors. An average working day is between twelve to fourteen hours. Since there is a shortage of power and most small units cannot afford generators, work continues through the night. The thekedar or unit owner decides what constitutes a working day. If units are not operating because of electricity breakdown, then the working day (that is the number of hours that constitutes a working day) stretches out way into the night.

After the third year, the child starts earning Rs 150-250 a month if he is about twenty-five to twenty-six years of age that he may be able to earn as much as Rs 500-600 But, as the workers pointed out, after working under such conditions, very few are able to manage a twelve-hour shift. Within a matter of six to seven years, that is by the time a child is thirteen or fourteen years old, he is afflicted by tuberculosis, bronchitis, asthma and other diseases.

PROCESSES IN THE LOCK INDUSTRY AND PARTICIPATION OF CHILDREN

Children are employed to work on hand-presses which cut different components of locks. Of all the processes in which children are employed, the activities of polishing, electroplating, spray painting and working on hand-presses are the most hazardous for the health of workers, particularly child workers. The hand-presses become particularly dangerous because children are made to work very long hours-anything from twelve to fourteen hours a day. Carelessness caused by exhaustion is the main cause of accidents and often, children lose the tips of their fingers, which get caught in the machines.

Polishing on buffing Machines

The work of polishing is perhaps the most hazardous job undertaken Rusted pieces of metal are polished on buffing machines. The bobs on these machines against the bob and the rusted portion is polished off. The face of the worker is within ten inches of rotating machines which run on power. The worker is bent over and directly inhales the emery powder and metal dust. Polishers can easily be identified because they look like coal-miners. They are covered from head to toe in this black powder. If a piece slips from the hand of the worker, it can severely injure another worker.

I visited about fifty such polishing units where more than 60 per cent of the workers were less than fourteen years of age. Children of eight and nine years could be seen working very late at night. I saw some children sleeping on the premises and some eating there as well. There were no exhaust fans in any of the units. Children who were too young to work on the machines could be seen gumming discs and then covering them with the black masala (as this mix is called. It is a term used to describe a mix of ingredients). This process generates a lot of dust and therefore factory owners keep buffing machines in a separate place.

Most factories in the industrial area had a separate place where buffing machines were kept. But factory owners felt that they were not responsible for the working conditions as the machines and the space were given on rent to the contractor, who hired the labour.

While large factories have their own buffing machines, most of the polishing work is done in the Upper Kote mohallas. This is where there is a maximum concentration of such unregulated units. Most of them are unregistered and there is on control over working g conditions, hours of work or wages. In the lanes and by-lanes of Upper Kote, child labour is very visible. In many buffing units I visited, more than 70 per cent of the workers were children. Buffing units are also found in the khirni Gate area and in the other parts of the city, but the highest concentration is in the Upper Kote area.

Electroplating

Electroplating is another extremely hazardous process in which more than 70 per cent of workers are children below the age of fourteen years. These children are engaged in tying polished metal pieces on copper wires, which are then strung on rods and submerged in acid and alkaline baths. In many of the units I visited (approximately fifty), it was not possible to enter the premises because of the noxious fumes which also made one's eyes water. Electroplating is hazardous for a variety of reasons. For one thing. the chemicals used such as potassium cyanide, trisodium phosphate, sodium silicate, hydrochloric acid, sulphuric acid, sodium hydroxide, chromic acid and barium hydroxide are extremely dangerous. The hands of children were in these solutions for the better part of a twelve-hour day, if not longer. Secondly, an electric current passes through these chemical tanks and children often get shocks. The floors of these units were wet and accidents were frequent.

Although most units had a convertor, which transformed AC current into DC current and though the current passed did not exceed ten volts, illegal electricity connections taken from street-lights made this extremely dangerous. There were cases of electrocution.

Electroplating units can be found in all parts of the city though they are concentrated in the Upper Kote area. In none of the units did workers wear gloves of aprons and there were no exhaust fans installed anywhere. Many of the smaller units were run by people who had worked in a supervisory capacity in larger factories, saved money or taken loans and then set up their own units. Every single unit owner interviewed said that he would not allow his on own children to even go near the unit Their children were all in local schools. But these very owners used child labour because they admitted that it was cheaper than employing adults. Many units were working at night as well.

Spray Painting

At least 50 per cent of the total labour force in the spray painting units observed was made up of children below the age of fourteen years. They were engaged in placing pieces of metal on trays which they then carried to the painting table. They were also employed to pass on pieces to the man who held the spray gun. In this process, they inhaled substantial quantities of paint and paint thinners. Many children were found working beyond midnight.

HAZARDS TO HEALTH

Polishing

Fazal Ahmed is thirty-five years, and has been working on a buffing machine for ten years. Now his two sons have also started working. Ahmed said that almost all polishers suffer from chest disorders, particularly tuberculosis. polishers inhale vast quantities of metal dust and emery powder in the course of their work and consequently find if very difficult to swallow. Another worker said that after a few years, polishers also find it difficult to breathe. I met two boys, eight and twelve respectively, both of whom were working as polishers and who already had TB

Electroplating

One electroplating unit owner, Nabi Ahmed, had himself worked for twenty years in an electroplating plant. Although most workers were abjectly poor, some were able to set up small units but could not afford to hire labour.1 Now about forty-five to fifty years old, Nabi Ahmed had a severe asthmatic condition and could hardly breathe. He has stopped working and employs others. On being asked whether his children were working, his answer was ; So long as I am alive, I will never let my children work. Look at my condition. I cannot even breathe easily. I do not let may children even enter the premises. Both my boys aged seven and nine years are studying.'

However, Nabi Ahmed has to employ other children if he wants to make enough money to avoid having his own children work. But that is described as duniya dari (ways of the world)

Nabi Ahmed said that electroplating work is very dangerous. He recalled the case of a child who, by accident, put some potassium cyanide in his mouth thinking it was salt and died instantaneously. Ever so often a child tastes some of the liquid in the chemical tanks out of curiosity, as small children tend to do, and gets seriously ill or dies. But there is no one who can say exactly how many deaths, accidental or otherwise, take place

Gyan Prakash, aged thirty-five (though he looked older), worked for several years in the Tiger Lock Factory near Marris Road. They had a big electroplating plant in which he was a supervisor and was responsible for mixing chemicals in solution with potassium cyanide and dissolved it with his hands, eating; the minute he took a break and washed his hands before eating; the minute he put the food in his mouth, he started vomiting blood. He vomited four of five times and was rushed to the Employees State Insurance Corporation(ESIC) Hospital, He was ill for a long time and never went back to work. He think that perhaps the glove was lightly torn and some chemicals had stuck to his nails and these did not come off with washing.

Gyan Prakash has worked in several karkhanas but he finds it hard to work in electroplating units. The smell of acids gives him a headache and he is unable to eat. Now he works only in a supervisory capacity in this unit. He has three children who go to school. He does not want his children to work so long as he can work. and particularly so for children. As he said, 'Although every child who comes to work is warned not to put his fingers in his mouth, children are, after all, children. How can I keep such vigil? But we know that potash (potassium cyanide) is used and we have to be careful.

This is not the end of the story. Liquids in these tanks are heated, and strong fumes are inhaled by adults and children alike. Many workers, both adults and children, work continuously for days on end, night and day. As another worker said: 'Maalik ko to kaam se matlab hein. Admi mare ya jiye, usko kya farak padta hein.? (the owner is only interested in the profit margin. What difference does it make to him if the worker lives or dies?)

In the electroplating plants, hazards to health arise not only from the acids and alkalies used but also from electricity. In Tan Tan Para, a mohalla in Upper Kote. an eleven-year old worker was recently electrocuted when his foot touched a naked wire. The poor wiring system, the presence of water and illegal connections from street-lights are the main reasons for people being electrocuted or receiving severe shocks, One adolescent youth complained of severe problems of breathlessness ever since he received an electric shock. Another electroplating unit worker said that in his work-place, a worker had been saved in the nick of time. Two wires got joined together and the nickel bath got electrified. The young worker of about fifteen or sixteen was arranging wires on the rods. He was unconscious for a long time.

Workers, whether polishers, painters or electroplanters, say that a lot depends on what can afford to eat. If he is able to get decent food, milk, butter and so on, he can ward off illness more easily. Otherwise it is a downhill path. Needless to say, those who work in these units cannot afford to eat well.

Spray Painting

A painter working for last fifteen years in a spray painting unit, started his work at the age of ten. After five or six years of working twenty hours at a stretch, he found that his body would get very hot and he felt like hitting someone. He said that this went on for five or six years. He was always close to losing his temper and many times he felt that he was close to murdering someone. according to him, this was a physiological condition and not just a psychological state. He could actually feel the blood rushing to his head. Finally, he left the job because he felt that he might not be able to control himself. He thinks that this was due to the combined impact of paint thinners, the bright lights, the heat of the ovens and the long hours of work. he was alright soon after he changed the job. Now he has set his own spray painting unit where he employed both children and adults. He plans to remove his own son to do some other work.

8

The Child Potters of Khurja

William Wood, 9 years old, 'was 7 years 10 months old when be began to work.' He 'ran mould' (carried ready-moulded articles into drying-room, afterwards bringing back the empty mould) from the very beginning. He came to work every day in the week at 6 a.m., and left off at about 9 p.m. 'I work till 9 o'clock at night six days in the week . I have done so for the last seven or eight weeks. ' Fifteen hours of labour for a child of 7! J.Murray, 12 years of age, says: 'I turn jigger and run mould. I come at 6. Sometimes I come at 4. I worked all night last night, till 6 o'clock this morning. I have not been in bed since the night before last. There were eight or nine other boys working last night. All but one have come this morning. I get 3 shillings and six pence. I do not get any more for working at night. I worked two nights last week.' Fernybough, a boy of 10: I have not always an hour (for dinner). I have only half an hour sometimes: on Thursday, Friday, and Saturday.' (Karl Marx quoting from the Children's Employment Commission, First Report of 1863 describing the conditions of children working in the pottery industry of England).

THE POTTERY INDUSTRY OF KHURJA

Children in the pottery industry of Khurja today do exactly the same work as children did in nineteenth-century England. Their work is described locally as uthai rakhai (pick up and put down). They carry empty moulds to the worker who works on the jigger jolly and carry the filled moulds out in the sun to dry. The boys who do this work are called phantiwalas (the boys who carry the phanti which is a piece of wood on which five or six moulds are kept). About 95 per cent of all working children in Khurja are phantiwalas. The only difference in the conditions of children in the pottery industry today and in nineteenth-century England is that they work not more than nine or ten hours a day and rarely do night-work.

The pottery industry of Khurja is over 600 hundred years old and is considered to be the traditional occupation of the people of Khurja in Bulandshar district of Uttar Pradesh. It may be clarified here than when people speak of pottery being a traditional industry of Khurja, they are really referring to the few families of Multani Kumbhars (potters) who came with the Mughal armies. The local village potter, part and parcel of Indian rural society, is not included in this description.(Burra 1987c).

There are almost 20,000 workers engaged either directly or indirectly in the pottery industry. Of the total workers,approximately 5000 or 25 percent are children below the age of fourteen years. However, these are only estimates and no-one is sure of the actual figures. But factory owners say that the total work-force within the factories is 6000 adults and a few hundred women and children. They arrive at these figures by calculating at the rate of nine workers in each factory and there are officially about 500 pottery units. But a study of about 25 per cent of the units revealed that except for a handful of units where there were less than ten workers, 90 per cent of them had more than twenty-five workers each with about 25 per cent of the work-force being made up of children below the age of fourteen years. Some units had almost eight to ninety workers employed.

The pottery industry of Khurja makes a variety of ceramic goods such as flower vases, object d'art,crockery, industrial ceramics like chemical porcelain, ball mill linings and balls, electrical and electronic ceramics like low tension(L.T.) and high tension (H.T.) insulators, spark plugs, sanitary ware,stone-ware jars, etc. Crockery and insulators account for the major share of what is produced.

The annual turn-over of the Khurja pottery industry is Rs.8 crores (Bhattacharya 1982). If these are the official figures, I was told in Khurja that actual production is three times what is declared and the estimate is deliberately kept low in order to evade excise. Individual units purposely show turnover figures of less than Rs. 7.5 lakhs to claim exemption from excise and retain their classification in the small-scale sector.

Other important pottery centres in Uttar Pradesh are located At Chinhat, Chuna, Basti and Ghaziabad.

I visited more than forty-nine units where pottery was being made in factories, ten units where work was being done exclusively with help of family labour, ten units where, in addition of family labour, some hired help was also used and eight families or rural potters who did not made the famous Khurja pottery but were exclusively involved with supplying pots for the local market. I spent nineteen days in Khurja. I was able to interview people from different segments of the pottery industry: hundred workers-me, women and children-twenty factory owners, eight thekedars (contractors), five master craftsmen, five traders, two doctors and a few government officials.

THE KHURJA POTTERY INDUSTRY : GENESIS AND DEVELOPMENT

Khurja is a small town located in the Bulandshar district of western Uttar Pradesh. It is hemmed in on both sides by the rivers Ganga and Yamuna, which flow at a distance of forty-five kilometers. It is approximately eighty-three kilometers by road from Delhi. Khurja junction is well connected by rail, situated as it is on the main Delhi-Howrah railway line. Thus it is very conveniently connected with some of the major towns and cities of India both by road and by rail.

The Khurja pottery industry has a long history. It is believed that Timur Lang, who sacked Delhi in 1398, had a band of soldiers amongst whom were also skilled potters. These potters stayed back and settled down in Multan (now in Pakistan) and near Delhi.1 They were adept at making blue pottery with Persian designs and colours. About 600 years ago, in reign of Mohammad Bin Tughlak, some of the potters' families moved from Delhi to Khurja (Bhattacharya 1982:8;Sharma 1978:208). They started with red clay pottery and then went on to introduce blue glazes on redclay articles with an englobe or coating of white clay, painting floral designs with cupric oxide and applying a soft glaze containing glass, red lead, quartz and borax. The basic raw material was the locally available red clay.

At first the traditional potters made hookahs (pipes), surahis (water-containers) and vessels as well as decorated wares. They attracted the attention of the outside world when two of the master potters from Khurja were invited to the Coronation Exhibition in London in 1911 to demonstrate their skill on the potter's wheel. The grandson of one of the master potters, Rasheed Ahmed, is one of the leading master potters of Khurja and has recently won the master craftsman's award.

Until the 1930s, the pottery industry of Khurja was the preserve of two families of Multani Kumbhars. In 1934, in order to develop the pottery industry the Government of Uttar Pradesh took the initiative and sent Professor H.N.Ray of the Banaras Hindu University to investigate the feasibility of making white-ware goods using modern technology and newer raw white-ware goods using modern technology and newer raw materials such as China clay, feldspars and quartz. The local potters were quite receptive to the new methods. But their activities did not make much headway till World War II.

The Second World was largely instrumental in giving a boost to the ceramic industry because there was a ban on use of various metal for making household utensils. During the war, import of ceramic goods was drastically curtailed and to meet the demand of ceramic goods was drastically curtailed and to meet the demand of ceramic wares for the war hospitals, the Uttar Pradesh government set up a factory in Khurja in 1942 for making such articles under the supervision of H.N.Ray. When the war was over, the factory had to be closed down in 1946 due to lack of demand for the products. It was decided then to convert the factory which had three small kilns, two chimneys and three ball mills into the Pottery Development Centre. The workers of the now defunct factory were provided with alternative employment. They were given the processed body and other raw materials from the Centre and were also allowed the facility of firing their green wares or unbaked ;goods in government kilns on payment of a nominal rent. This Centre is the first Common Facility Centre in the country and the main cause for the development of the Khurja pottery industry.

The Centre started in 1946 with only eight potters. Initially,it was purely a cottage industry producing cheap quality products which had a limited market. In 1953, Dr.T.N.Sharma, a ceramic expert, sent to Japan for training. On his return in 1955, he demonstrated the use of better technology using local raw materials. he also improved the jigger jolly machines and the shape of saggars (fire resistant containers in which unbaked pots are baked) and was primarily responsible for a number of schemes for the development of the pottery industry under the Second Five-Year Plan.

the Khurja pottery industry today has three types of entrepreneurs. The oldest are master craftsmen, also known as traditional potters, who have adapted to the new technology and now make their art-ware largely with the help of the new technology using the terra cotta moulds rather than the potter's wheel. But they have not given up their old methods of decoration, painting and glazes.

The Second type of entrepreneur is the one who learnt the skills offered by the Pottery Development Centre and set up his own unit. And the third type of entrepreneur is the person who had the finance to set up his units but has not actually learnt the job himself. Interestingly, the traditional village potter has not entered the industry. He continues his traditional work for a totally different market and is not included in the list of Khurja potters. By definition, the Khurja potter makes his wares for an outside market, while the local village potter produces to meet local needs.

The pottery industry in Khurja was set up because it was felt that there was a tradition of pottery in the area and a market for the goods. The people who were pioneers in this industry, like Dr. Sharma, had envisaged that by setting up an industry and providing facilities, many people would get employment here. In face, in the early years, the training was very rigorous and those who wanted to set up independent units had to prove their knowledge and ability, for the facilities provided by the government were crucial for their economic upliftment. But in later years the pottery industry developed independently:many people seeing the potential of the industry set up units without actually knowing the work just because it was a good business proposition. Today, therefore, there is not much similarity amongst the different types of entrepreneurs.

A common complaint of traders or financiers-turned-entrepreneurs is that the skilled worker-turned-entrepreneur has ruined the market because of his lack of knowledge, illiteracy and absence of financial staying power. Many of the smaller entrepreneurs are heavily indebted to local dealers who are making all the profits. The worker-turned-entrepreneur knows so little about the business side of pottery that he has knows so little about the business side of pottery that he has no idea of the true value of his goods at a low price. Since the goods produced in all the factories are, quality-wise, almost on par with each other, the financier-turned-entrepreneur is not able to make as large a profit as he would like to. The result has been that a large a profit as he would like to. The result has been that a cartel of them has started marketing their own goods in order to bypass the local dealers. So great is the resentment against the skilled worker-turned-entrepreneur that these educated entrepreneurs, some years ago, tried to force the government to pass a resolution that coal quotas would only be given to those units which had a certain area of factory,size of kiln and quantum of capital. The idea was to displace the small entrepreneur but it did not succeed.

THE POTTERY INDUSTRY TODAY STRUCTURE AND MARKET

There are four types of pottery units in Khurja not including the local potter who produces red clay goods for the local market. Most of the other pottery units produce for the outside market. Out of a total of almost 500 units,less than 50 per cent actually function. The reason is the large-scale black-marketing of coal, which is the primary raw material need in this industry. Workers told this researcher that small unit owner could easily earn Rs.10,000 a month by just a black-marketing coal and was also saved the problems of actually running a unit. Out of the 500 units that are registered with the Government Pottery Centre, approximately 300 are run by traders, twenty-five by traditional potters and seventy-five units belong to skilled workers who have save money and set up on their own. About hundred units belong to people who have received training in the manufacture of pottery but who no longer use their own hands.

Looked at from another point of view, the units in the industry could be classified differently. The first and largest category is made up of independent pottery units, which are equipped with their own machinery and manufacture their own processed clay called body and glazes and have their own forming and firing facilities. Some of them also do decoration work on their products. There are 398 such units.

The second category consists of dependent units which have no processing and firing facilities of their own. They obtain the processed body,glazes and other raw material from outside, make the green wares at their units and after applying the glazes, get the wares fired at the kilns provided by the Uttar Pradesh Small Industries Corporation potteries Ltd. and pay a nominal rent. There are 126 registered dependent potters in Khurja.

There are twenty units which only manufacture the processed body and glazes and sell them to the dependent units which do not have these facilities. While the Government Centre is supposed to do this, dependent potters require credit which the Centre cannot provide and there private manufacturers area able to do good business. There are also units which only undertake the decoration of pottery articles on a piece-rate or job work basis. There are twenty such registered units.

Another category of potter who makes clay goods in Khurja is formed by the local potters who do not make goods for outside market, but only for the local market. There are colonies of the local Kumbhar in the city and in the surrounding villages who make large containers for water and grain, Kulhads (clay cups) which are sold to halwais (sweetmeat sellers) and sakuras (small plates) bought for feasts and weddings. These traditional potters also make plates which are no longer in demand because of plastic and paper goods.

In a recent report on the development of the ceramic industry in India, it was estimated that there would be a crockery demand of 33 million sets during the Seventh Five-year plan period. It is estimated that the demand for clay-based crockery from the urban sector would be 1,28,500 tonnes. According to the 1985 figures, 10,700 tonnes were produced in the organized sector and 71,000 in the small-scale sector. Of these all-India figures, the contribution of the Khurja units was 15,000 tonnes or more than 20 per cent of all the crockery produced in the small-scale sector in India. The small-scale sector, under which the Khurja pottery industry falls, supplies mostly stoneware items to people with little purchasing power. The middle-class purchaser is fed by both the small-scale and the organized sector manufacturer of quality stoneware, earthenware, etc., and the higher economic strata buy superior bone china products. Khurja makes about 50 per cent of low tension insulators in the country and about 10 per cent of kit-kats. The only sanitary goods made in Khurja are foot-rests for Indian-style toilets.

While the demand for pottery is very high and growing, the goods produced by the local village have less demand than before. The village potter in Khurja is facing competition from plastic, paper and dried leaf plated and bowls. As one potter said:

> There is at least a 25 per cent fall in the demand for our goods even in the local villages because of the paper and plastic plates and saucers. Even though our goods are cheaper, there is more prestige in using plastic goods and these have become status symbols.

The local potter who uses the red clay locally available has not made any advance in technology from the government. The Khadi and village Industries Commission, which was set up to help village artisans, introduced white-ware pottery in the villages instead of promoting local methods. This venture failed miserably for a host of reasons: there was no market in the villages for these goods, the village potter did not have resources for raw material or fuel and, in any case, could not find avenues for selling the goods produced.

PROCESS IN THE POTTERY INDUSTRY

In most of the big ceramic units, the raw material is processed on the premises with the help of machines called jaw crushers, edge runners, clay blunger,etc. The processes in the pottery industry of Khurja are many depending upon the goods made. One commonly used method is by throwing clay on the potter's wheel. This is the traditional method of making red clay potteries throughout India. In Khurja, the traditional potters even now use the kick-wheels for making decorated potteries. The potters uses his hand pressure to shape the body. This process is wholly manual.

Another method is known as the beating or patting method. This consists of formation of clay-ware by beating a roughly thrown piece of leather-hard clay with a wooden beater to the required shape and thickness. This process reduces the porosity of the clay body and makes it homogeneous and strong. In Khurja, this process is used only for making the saggars or containers in which the unbaked clay goods are put before firing the kilns. The saggar body is put on the outside of a wooden frame and beaten into the required shape and thickness by a wooden beater.

Most of the crockery, plates, cups and saucers, etc., are shaped on the jigger and jolly machines. The jigger and jolly process is used to produce hollow single shapes on a mass scale. A jigger consists of a vertical shaft having a cup-shaped wheel-head which receives the mould made by plaster of paris. It is mostly power-driven and is provided with a foot-brake. Some units produce jiggered items without using power, by pedaling. A jolly consists of an inclined arm mounted on a pivot with a balancing counterpoise on one arm. The opposite arm carries a profile which is an iron tool to give shape to the article. Depending upon the goods being made, a quantity of clay is put into the mould fitted to the head and pressed to shape by the profile by lowering the arm of the jolly. For every article, a separate mould is fixed to the jigger head.

All the ceramic units a Khurja making crockery use this process. This technique, however, cannot make the complete product. Handles for teapots, jugs, etc.are made by the slip casting and then joined to these articles.

For slip casting, a plaster of paris mould is made and the slip which consists of a semi-viscous slurry of the ceramic body is poured into it. The excess liquid is poured out after some time. The inside of the mould becomes covered with a thin layer of the body after the water is soaked by the plaster mould. After some time,the layer becomes hard and is removed from the mould. It is then finished by scraping off the extra clay, smoothened with fine sandpaper and, finally, with a soft wet sponge. This method is also used for making complicated shapes such as soup spoons. In Khurja, this method is widely used for making both chemical porcelain as well as crockery and tableware.

The slip is made from finely ground plastic body by adding small amounts of sodium silicate or sodium carbonate to act as deflocculent. For both the slip method and the jigger jolly method, units make their own mould of plaster of paris. But not more than three or four castings can be done from one mould efficiently. Making articles of complicated shapes or large sizes requires the use of several mould for making the component parts which are subsequently joined.

Pressing in steel dies using hydraulic presses is used of making tiles and high-tension electro-porcelain. One tile manufacturing unit and a few high-tension insulator units (up to 11 KVA) At Khurja are using this technique. The technique is also being used by other units for making electrical kit-kats, technical ceramics and other products of simple shapes. Small articles are being made by hand presses.

In the organized sector, the green-wares are dried in rooms using a hot blast of air. But by and large, drying is done in the shade by keeping the green-wares on the floor outside or by stacking them in shelves for a few days. Once the goods are dried they are scraped for any rough edges and smoothened with water. If they are hand-painted or decorated otherwise, they are given over to the painter and decorators. The dried goods not painted are sent for direct glazing.

The earliest of Khurja used indigenous red clay for their goods. But today all the raw material comes from outside. The china clay comes from Rajmahal in Bihar, Ahmedabad in Gujarat, Chandia in Madhya Pradesh and Bikaner in Rajasthan. The ball clay is available only in Rajasthan, Andhra Pradesh, Gujarat and Kerala. The feldspars comes from Rajasthan and quartz comes from Rajasthan, Andhra Pradesh, Gujarat and Madhya Pradesh. The main source of fuel, coal, comes from the collieries of the eastern coal fields situated in Bihar and West Bengal. The independent units get their coal against allotment directly from the mines. The dependent units are allotted the requisite quantity of coal from the coal dump of the pottery Development Centre for firing in the rented kilns.

Glazes are homogeneous mixtures of silicate minerals and chemicals which melt to form glass and are used to provide a lustrous coating to the porous fired products to render them impervious. They fit the body intimately as the materials are mostly the same in both the bodies and the glasses. A ball mill us used to powder the glaze to the desired fineness.

The basic raw material for the unglazed pot are quartz, feldspars, plastic clay and china clay, marble or calcite, zinc oxide, barium carbonate, etc. In Khurja, mostly raw and opaque glasses are used which mature at medium temperatures. Different colouring oxides are used by Khurja potters for colouring glazes. Cobalt or copper oxide is used for all shades of blue and black. Copper and chrome oxide is used for the green colour. Iron oxide is used for giving the brown colour and manganese oxide is used for pink or violet colour. The traditional Khurja potters who have about twenty units now use commercially available glazes but some of them still prepare their own blue glazes and jealously guard the secret of their blue pottery.

The Khurja ceramic industry follows an intermediate level of technology. The wares are all single fired. Raw glazes insoluble in water are generally used. Barium glazes containing zirconia and /or titania as the opacifying agents are commonly used by the potters. The glazes is generally applied by dipping the dried green wares in the glaze slip. In some decorative wares, glazing is done by spraying. For various artistic designs, the colours are generally applied by hand painting by artist.

Once the goods are painted the glazed, they are baked in coal-fired, down-draught kilns. The kilns are of various sizes ranging from 2.4 metres (8 feet) to 7.3 metres (24 feet) in diameter. The wares are packed in saggars prevent direct contact of the wares with the flames and fumes of the fuel which would otherwise spoil the colour and glaze of the products. They also help to keep the glazed articles in position without sticking to each other. The temperature of the kiln is highest at the top, around 1250-1280 C for insulators and 1200-1500 C for crockery.

PARTICIPATION OF CHILDREN IN THE POTTERY INDUSTRY

The first job for the young child is to carry lumps of clay to the kataiwala (the worker who makes pots on the jigger jolly machine). Each Kataiwala has one or two helper, the phantiwalas, who are always children. Since this work is always done through a thekedar because the employer wants faster production. The work is done at a fantastic speed with both adults and children working at break-neck speed. An average kataiwala cuts 4000 pieces in an eight-hour shift and the phantiwala has to carry 4000 moulds outside in the open to dry to dry and carry back 4000 empty moulds to the kataiwala. In one factory, I noticed young children of nine and ten carrying six moulds on a phanti. The mould contained three-inch mugs, each of which contained 100 grams of clay. The mould itself weighed 300 grams. The combined weight of the moulds, the clay and the wood was about eight kilograms which the child carried on every trip. In an eight-hour day, he ran five kilometers a day at the very minimum with this load.

At another factory I saw children carry weight up to eleven kilograms on the phanti. I was told that on an average, the children made a thousand return trips in an eight-hour working day and covered a distance of six or seven kilometers. This was the work that children were mainly engaged in and their work was described as that of helpers!

This was not the only work that children did. Once the pots were partially dry, these children took out the half-dry pots and carried them to the workers who were engaged in finishing the work. In several factories, I noticed children stacking ninety mugs on a wooden platform and then carrying them on their heads to the adult workers. The weight of this burden, I was told by adult workers and factory owners, was more than ten kilograms. The children doing this work were so young that their hands and legs would tremble after they had put down the weight.

In one factory, I saw children unloading saggars, six at a time. Each saggar weighed half a kilogram. In one factory, a child of thirteen was carrying three saggars, each weighing eight kilograms. His body was bent double with the strain.

Another job that children are engaged in is removing handles from the moulds and carrying them to adults who finish them. some children were engaged in just cutting handles to the required size. On the average, they had to cut at least 3000-4000 pieces in an eight-hour shift. The children were engaged in the scraping of the rough edges from the mugs and other crockery pieces. Others helped with the final water finishing.

The children who have had a little experience work on

the jigger jolly machines, clean out the blunger machines and remove the pebbles from the processed clay. I saw children of ten, knee-deep in cold liquid clay, removing the large pebbles from the processed clay while the employer was standing outside the pit and giving instructions. children are also sent into slip pits to get liquid clay for the mould because adults do not like the work. It is taken for granted that children will clean the premises and do all the other menial tasks for which adults would be reluctant-such as running errands.

From village Bavanpur, approximately thirty-five workers come daily to work in potteries and these include eight or ten boys of the ages of ten to twelve years. Most of these children come from families of khet mazdoors (agricultural labourers). Some of them own two or three bighas (a unit for measuring land). The fathers of three boys also work in the pottery industry. Most of the children from this village belong to the caste of dhimar or thakur.

Sondha village is about fourteen kilometers from Khurja town and about hundred workers including thirty to forty boys and adolescents leave home daily at 7 a.m. to work in the potteries. Most of the parents working children have less than five bighas of land. Most of the families own one or two milch animals which the parents tend, while the children labour in the potteries. The parents of ten to fifteen boys also work in the potteries of Khurja. Interestingly, when I asked why children were being sent to work when there was so much adult unemployment, the answer that twenty-six-year old Manohar ram gave was: 'Many adults don's know how to cycle and even if they know, they don't own one. Children don't have that problem. They sit behind us and hitch a ride.'

Some of the children working in the potteries whom I had the opportunity to interview in depth seemed to be the sole earning members of their families. Kalu ram is twelve years old and comes daily from village Dharaon. He has no father and his mother keeps poor health. He has been working for the past five or six years and supports three younger brothers and two sisters. Vijay Pal and Hira Singh are thirteen years old. They are orphans and also come from Dharaon. Vijay Pal lives with his grandmother. He has no brothers and sisters. He started working in the potteries recently, and grazed the landlord's cattle before this. He said: 'In the villages, there is no work for children. We are expected to work without wages only for a little grain. My grandmother thought that it was about time I started bringing in a regular wage.'

Hira Singh has a brother who is the local quack. They have fifteen bighas of land. He studied up to the fifth standard and then his brother told him to start working.

Laxman Das is twelve years old and is a local Khurja boy. He and his younger brother, aged nine years, are the only earning members of their family. Laxman Das was embarrassed at being asked what his father did and said: 'He has retired.' He and his brother support a seven-member family. The contractor, who was standing nearby when I was interviewing Laxman Das, said: 'The man's a drunkard. The mother is lazy. They do not work because they have children to support them.

Ompal is fourteen years old. He started working a year back when he failed his sixth standard exam. It was also the time when his sister was getting married. He said:

My parent needed money for my sister's marriage so my brother and I started working in the potteries. I thought that after a while would go back to school but once you leave school, there is no going back. We still have sisters to settle. My parents have very little land.

I asked several children how they heard that work was available in the potteries. Fazal said:

Thekedars come to the villages and say they want children so we know that there is work. Often the thekedars don't want to give the work to adults. We are young, we can work fast and we don't get tired so easily.

Adults working in the pottery industry who took their children to work said: 'Our wages are so low that often we have no choice but to take our children to work to supplement the family income.' sometimes, as Karimbhai pointed out, a child has no aptitude for studying:

My boy is working in the factory with me. He is thirteen years old. When he failed his exams, I decided to put him to work. My other children are at school. If the boy is not studying, he might as well earn and pay for his own expenses.

But not all parents have this attitude. Savita, who has been working in the potteries for the last ten years, said:

My husband and I feel that we should not put our children to work at a young age. This is the age to play and run about, not to work in factories inhaling clay dust the whole day. We have decided that as long as we can manage, we won't send our children to work.

There are roughly speaking, three categories of children working in the pottery industry. The children of master crafts-men all have to learn the work of moulding clay on the traditional potter's wheel. But they do this work for a couple of hours in a day after school only because the parents feel that the child should know the technique even if he is later going to be managing the business and not doing the actual work. These children probably help out occasionally when the pressure of work is high but they are not regular workers. The number of children in this category in negligible since there are only two families of traditional potters who are master craftsmen today.

In the second category are children of skilled workers, mainly Biharis, who have set up their own units and run these exclusively using family labour. Here are children do not go to school but work full-time with their parents. This category of entrepreneur rarely employs hired labour and works solely with the help of his family. Such working children as described above probably account for about 5 per cent of the total child labour force.

In the third category are children who work full-time in factories doing the jobs described earlier. Occasionally, whole family is employed because there are small children who can help out with the work. But usually, children work alone. This type of working child accounts for more than 90 per cent of all children in the industry. Children working the potteries of Khurja were by and large illiterate. Many of them had studied up to the fourth standard but could barely read and write. While some children had left school because their parents wanted them to work, many children had failed their examination and the parents had felt that the child did not have an aptitude for studying and had withdrawn him from school.

One noticeable factor was that units producing quality goods did not employ child labour. Or only one or two children were present out of a total labour force of forty or fifty workers. Most of these units had tall racks next to the jigger jolly machines and the same adult worker would stack the phanti with the moulds on it. There was no need for a worker to run with the phanti. These units also came under the Factories Act and the owners said it was not worth their while to employ children when child labour was illegal in factories. Nor were children employed in units making insulators which require certain kind of skills. By and large, children are employed in units making crockery for bulk production.

While adult workers belong to almost all castes and communities, the children were either from Koli, Dhimar of Jatav families-Scheduled Castes or Muslims. I did not come across any children from high-caste families.

Most of the work that children do in the pottery industry can be done by adults as well. In fact in many factories, where children were not being employed, the same work was done by either adolescent boys or adults. But adult workers said:

We don't like this work because it is tiring. The body of

the child is supple and he can run fast, bend down and get up quickly without any problem. When you are older, it is difficult to do this work.

Factory owners and thekedars also said the same thing: 'If an adult is asked to do this work of fetching and carrying, he would take too long. Adults can't move with the speed that children can. It is not work meant for adults.'

WAGE STRUCTURE AND THE ORGANIZATION OF WORK

The wage structure is very flexible in the pottery industry. According to the Status Report on the ceramic industry at Khurja:

In the beginning very cheap labour was available at 50-75 paise per day for the skilled workers and 25-50 paise per day for unskilled one. The present wage of a skilled worker ranges from Rs 300-600 per month while an unskilled worker gets only Rs 150-300 per month. Jobs are generally done on piece rate basis but the pattern of income remains more or less the same. Cheap child labour is also abundantly available and utilized. Because of the low wages, ceramic industry has found a favorable labour pulled location at Khurja (Bhattacharya 1982:9).

As has been mentioned earlier, there are three types of pottery units. The traditional potters, who largely make art ware goods, supply them to boutiques in the major cities of India and to the five-star hotels. Their goods are quality goods and all the skilled work is done by members of their families but not that business has expanded, they do employ other workers-mainly painters-who get paid on a job basis and earn upto Rs 1500 a month. Many the them are art students who have got a BA degree as well. Their other workers earn about Rs 500 to Rs 600 a month and children earn on the average Rs 150-200 a month. Most of the work in these units is not done on contract because here it is important to maintain quality rather than increase quantity.

In the second category are those run mainly by Biharis using family labour and a few hired workers. Here the wages normally do not exceed Rs 300-500 a month for adults and less than Rs 200 for children.

The bulk of labour force is employed in independent units where they work on piece-rate wages. In every factory, there are a few workers who are employed on amani (monthly wages). But the majority of the workers are engaged by thekedars on piece-rate wages. Even those workers who are working on amani for many years are not considered permanent workers and such not entitled to any leave. On days the worker does not come, his wages are cut. In some factories where the workers have been able to fight for better conditions of work, the factory owner gives two paid holidays in a month. But in most factories this is not the practice and workers work seven days week without a break.

Since most of the workers are employed by the thekedars, the factory owner does not consider himself responsible for the workers. Many workers said that thekedars sometimes did not pay wages on time because they said the factory owner had not paid them or for some other reason. The thekedars some-factories cut the wages of the workers as commission. In most factories, a skilled worker earned not more than Rs. 400 a month and unskilled workers less than Rs.200 a month.

Many workers interviewed said that wages in the pottery industry were low because of the large influx of Bihari migrant labour. One worker said:

Most of these people belong to Gaya or Navada districts of Bihar. For them, it is impossible to earn even Rs 200 a month at home. When they are happy with their wages, then who is going to raise our wages?

Another adult worker, Ram Singh, said:

The factory owners know how to exploit these Biharis.

They offer them space in the factories to stay and coal to cook their food on. The Biharis are quite happy even though they get paid almost a hundred rupees less than the local adult workers for the same job.

Rafeeq, age forty, said:

These people work overtime without wages as a sign of gratitude to their employers. That is why they are employed.'

Different categories of workers were paid different wages. Some firemen said they were paid Rs 600; others said they were earning Rs 1100. Those earning monthly salaries earned more than those workers who were engaged by thekedars. Hardly any of the children interviewed earned more than Rs 150 a month for an eight-hour day.

Mulu Ram, all ow twelve, commuted daily from Dharaon, a village near Khurja. He started working five or six years ago at a daily wage of Rs 5 a day. Today, he earns Rs 8 a day as a phantiwala. He is the sole supporter of his family of five brothers and sisters and an ailing mother. If he works thirty days in a months, he earns Rs 150 a month.

Vijay Kashyap and Mira Singh, mentioned earlier, earn Rs. 180 a month if they work thirty days in a month and don't take any time off. They also work as phantiwalas. Laxmi Das and his eight-year old brother earn Rs 150 a month and between the two of them support a seven-member family.

In one unit I visited, one woman with three children between the ages of eight and ten was able to earn Rs 12 in an eight-hour day after finishing 1000 mugs.

By and large, the wages were as follows: the amani workers doing katai (wire on the jigger jolly machine) got Rs 500 a month, phantiwalas, if children, earned approximately Rs 150 a month but if they were older, they earned up to Rs 300 a month; those who fixed handles earned up to Rs 500; those who did finishing got Rs 300 a month. The workers who did finishing got Rs 300 a month. The workers who did glazing received Rs 400 a month. The workers on theka (contract) could earn as much in a month, they had to work twice as hard. Even the monthly wage workers had to complete a certain amount or work every day; otherwise, their salaries were cut but their work-load was not as heavy as that of contract labour.

In one factory, the workers told me that for scraping and water finishing the mugs, they got paid Rs 11 for 1000 pieces. Two people together could finish 2000 pieces on a day. Usually an adult would team up with a child and together they would do the work. It seemed that even individual workers tried to exploit children by making them work hard and then keeping a part of their wages for themselves as commission. This way, the adult worker could take it a little easy because the child would work harder. On contract labour, those who cut the handles earned approximately Rs 200 a month and those who joined the handles earned Rs 400 a month. To earn this much, the man had to work at breakneck speed and cut and fix 4000 pieces in eight hours.

Factory owners justifies the use of contract labour thus:

Workers on salaries become very lazy. An amani worker will cut only 2000 pieces on the jigger whereas the contract worker will cut 4000 pieces in eight hours. If you want production and increased profits, you cannot have salaried employees.

Mahesh, a work supervisor, said:

These maaliks (owners) are clever people. They want profit without responsibility for the workers. They is why 90 per cent of the work is done through thekedars. The factory owner then does not feel any responsibility for the labour. He fixes a rate with the thekedars and it is the responsibility of the thekedars to pay the labour.

The bulk of the work is done through sub-contracting though the work is all done in the factory premises. The general pattern is that the factory owner has a few adult workers on what is called amani or a monthly wage. They supervise the work of the thekedar and maintain quality. In some of the thekedar also helped out and thus saved on one adult's wage, the thekedar also helped out and thus saved on one adult's wage. It was the dream of every adult worker to become a thekedar. All the workers working under the thekedar were paid piece-rate wages. Since they were daily wages workers, no labour laws applied to them.

An interesting fact I observed was that worker who had started very young and worked for fifteen or twenty years earned exactly the same amount as the new adult entrants. The reason for this state of affairs, I was told was:

If you start working young mentality changes and you lose all purpose in life except to carry on with whatever you get. There is no fight left in you so you don't ask for your just dues. That's why employers prefer children. Also, you have to be really desperate in the first place to start work so young and the spirit is beaten out of you by the time you are an adult. Those who start working as adults earn more than those who started off as children.

HEALTH HAZARDS

In England in the nineteenth-century, writes Karl Marx, the pottery industries were amongst the hazardous for the health of the workers. The Children's Employment Commission Report of 1863 drew attention to the kinds of health hazards faced by workers in the potteries of Stoke-on-Trent and Wolstanton. Marx, using the reports of the public health committees, has this to say:

Dr. Greenhow states that the average life-expectancy in the pottery districts of Stoke-on-Trent and Wolstanton is extraordinarily low. Although only 36.6 per cent in the potteries in the district of Stoke, and 30.4 per cent in Wolstanton,more than half the death among men of that age in the result of pulmonary diseases among the potters. Dr Boothroyd, a medical practitioner at Hanley, say: 'Each successive generation of potters is more dwarfed and less robust than the proceeding one. 'Similarly another doctor, Mr McBean states: 'Since I began to practice among the potters 25 years ago,I have observed a marked degeneration, especially shown in diminutions of stature and breadth.' These statements are taken from Dr Greenhow's Report of 1860 (Marx [1867] 1982).

Further he writes:

Dr J.T. Arledge, senior physician of the North Staffordshire Infirmary, says: 'The potters as a class, both men and women, represent a degenerated population, both physically and morally. They are, as a rule, stunted in growth, ill-shaped, and frequently ill-formed in the chest;they become prematurely old, and are certainly short-lived; they are phlegmatic and bloodless, and exhibit their debility of constitution by obstinate attacks of dyspepsia, and disorders of the liver and kidney, and by rhenumatism, to pneumonia, phthisis, bronchitis, and asthma. One form would appear peculiar to them, and is known as potter's asthma, or potter's consumption.

While it may seem as if the work of uthai rakhai is not apparently hazardous because it is merely carrying pots from one place to another it is the total environment which makes the industry hazardous. According to Dr N.C.Saxena,the Hospital Superintendent at the local Khurja hospital,most potters who come to the hospital at the local Khurja hospital,most potters who come to the hospital had asthmatic bronchitis, which then became tuberculosis. Out of 300 tuberculosis patients registered at the hospital for regular care, 70 per cent were potters. In his own experience of two years, there have been four or five patients with silicosis. According to Dr Saxena: four or five patients with silicosis. According to Dr Saxena:

If we have got 300 patients in our hospital, there would be another 700 patients being treated outside by private practitioners and quacks. But most of the patients must be going undiagnosed. There are at least two or three patients with asthmatic bronchitis in every pottery. The children working in potteries suffer from extra pulmonary tuberculosis and out of every ten, one has pulmonary tuberculosis.

Dr Saxena has been trained to identify silicosis but most of the local doctors treat it as tuberculosis. Silicosis is a pulmonary fibrosis caused by the inhalation of dust containing free silica. It is the most common and severe of all pneumoconiosis. It is basically a nodular fibrosis of the lungs. The lungs' vital capacity is reduced and the patient dies. There is no cure for silicosis which has now been identified as an occupational disease.

Dr Masood Ahmed runs a clinic in the centre of the town. Most of his patients are potters. He gets on the average twenty-five or thirty adult potters a day and an equal number of children. The most common complaint of his patients is asthmatic bronchitis and pulmonary tuberculosis. Out of 200 patients he had recently examined, 75 per cent were potters and 87.5 per cent of them had pulmonary tuberculosis, bronchitis and asthma. According to him:

By the time the potter is thirty to thirty-five years old, the upper respiratory infection has gone into the third stage. By the age of forty or forty-five, the man dies. Most of the workers are too poor to take treatment. Many of them do not get paid regularly. We advise rest but that is impossible for them.

According to the International Labour Organization Encyclopedia on Occupational Health and Safety (Parmeggiani 1983, the silicosis hazard is encountered in a wide variety of occupations including the manufacture of pottery, porcelain, refractory materials, etc. 'Cough with sputum, is an indication of bronchitis, and chronic bronchitis is frequently associated with advanced silicosis.' The three main complications of silicosis are also the most frequent causes of death and those are pulmonary tuberculosis, respiratory insufficiency and acute pulmonary infection. According to the above-mentioned encyclopedia:

Pulmonary tuberculosis is,even today, still the cause of death in a quarter of cases, and is the most request complication. It has recently been proved that tubercle bacilli grow and multiply far more actively in macroplages that have phagocytised silica particles than in those that have not done so, perhaps because the former have suffered a loss of vitality and are no longer capable of destroying the tubercle bacilli.

There are specific hazards in the pottery industry. According to same encyclopedia: 'Ball clay contains up to 50% free silica and so presents a potential hazard to sliphouse workers handling raw clay.

Further, it is stated:

The major health hazard is pneumoconiosis, which results from the prolonged inhalation of siliceous dust within the respirable size range, that is, particles up to about 7 micro m in diameter. The risk arises from the combination of materials and methods and is proportional to the percentage of free silica in the inhaled dust; in general, it is confined to the pre-firing processes.

These are not the only health hazards faced by workers but these are the most common ones. Workers who work as firemen at the kiln, lose their eyesight, I was told, by the age of about forty-five or so. Their main job is to stoke the fire and to periodically remove samples of pottery to check whether they have been properly baked. as workers said: 'Ankhon ko aach lag jati hai' (the eyes get affected by the heat). Those who work on the ball machines become deaf after some time. Children complained of frequent coughs and colds. The main reason, as one child told me, was: 'Selkhari se nazla ho jata hai' (soap stone dust causes cold.) Most of the workers who were affected by silicosis were those working on disintegrators. These were machines used to powder the broken saggars for re-use. In fact, most factories had this process not in their main area but outside because of the dust that flew out. But operators of the machines were affected.

When workers interviewed in the factories, they said that the work was not hazardous. Part of the reason for this is that colds and coughs are not considered illnesses and no one wants to admit that they have tuberculosis. In fact, local doctors said they had no idea what happened to many of their patients as the minute a person heard that he had T.B., he would rarely come back to them. Most doctors, therefore, in order to keep their custom did not tell the patient that he suffered from T.B. but gave him whatever relief they could give.

Workers in Sondha village said that it was not uncommon to hear about accidental deaths in potteries. The main explanation offered was bad house-keeping on the part of the factory owners. A young adolescent, Birpal, recently died in a factory because the belts which rotate the grinding machines broke and he was trapped. Birpal's family was of course not compensated. Some workers said: Bachaon ko slip ke tank me bhej dete hein. Kai bacche thandi se behosh ho jate hein'(They put children into the slip tanks and some children become unconscious because of the extreme cold).

This was verified by Dr Ahmed as well who told me that one of his patients had even gone into a coma because of this experience. Other workers in the village said that often working for some years in the potteries: Dum ghut jaata hai' (One starts suffocating).

While there is substantial documentary evidence that pottery is hazardous work because of the large-scale use of silica which is one of the essential raw materials used, most workers interviewed at the factories did not complain of any health problems. Cold and cough and slight breathing difficulties were common but were not taken seriously by the workers themselves. It seems that not all workers in the pottery industry are exposed to health hazards because many are working with wet clay so there is a minimum of dust in the air. However, those workers directly grinding the raw material would be the most affected. This is also a relatively new industry and the impact of the working conditions on the health of workers may only manifest itself at a later stage.

LABOUR LAWS AND THEIR IMPLEMENTATION

Under the Factories Act of 1948, which also applies to Uttar Pradesh, a factory means any premises where ten or more workers are working, or were working on any day of the preceding twelve months, and where in any part of which a manufacturing process is being carried out with the aid of power. If any manufacturing unit has more than ten workers, they are supposed to provide certain facilities to their employees such as rest-rooms, drinking water facilities, toilets, etc. Workers are not supposed to be employed beyond a certain number of hours a week without being paid overtime. There is a strict ban on the employment of children in factories under the age of fourteen years.

In order to evade the Factories Act, 90 per cent of the units show that they have less than nine workers. In some factories I visited, I noticed around fifty workers. But when I asked the employer, he said there were only eight people working there! In every singly factory I visited, there were over twenty workers employed and the factory owners made no bones about the fact that they were breaking the law. As one factory owner said:

If there are more than nine worker, then we come under the purview of the Factory Act. This a nuisance because we have to give bonus and provide employees medical insurance, etc. That is why we show fewer workers. But this was not an isolated response. Every single factory owner in Khurja I interviewed told me the same thing. Workers felt bitterly about it and said: 'Factory inspectors come. Labour inspectors come. They take money and go away. Who cares about labour?

Every where t talked to workers, the story was the same. Some worker said that one of the reasons why the industry was listed as cottage and small-scale industry was because this sector was exempt form excise duty. One worker said:

The factory owners make twice as much as they show in books. All of them have two books. This way they have double benefit. They claim that there are only nine worker so that they do not come under the purview of the Factories Act. But you must have seen that this is a lie. There is no job security here and that is why there is so much child labour. Everyone in Khurja-workers, employers, contractors and traders-were aware that under the Factories Act,child labour is expressly forbidden. When I first visited Khurja and talked to people, everyone denied that child labour existed. But when I showed them photographs of working children, they said that the reason for their denial was because there was a ban on the employment of children under the Factories Act.

Many factory owners expressed the view that the main reason that there was no progress in the country was that there were labour laws. One factory owner said: 'You can either have production or you can look after the welfare of workers. Isn't it enough that we people are giving the poor employment? Why do we need laws to protect them as well?'

Soon after this study was published in a local newspaper, there were questions in Parliament. The reply of the then Minister for Labour was that it was the State Government's responsibility to enforce the Factories Act and the Child Labour (Prohibition and Regulation) Act,1986. He admitted in Parliament that although the Labour Ministry had received an unofficial report (mine) about child labour in the pottery industry of Khurja, the State Government maintained there was not a single case of child labour to be found in this industry! (Times of India,26 March 1988). When the author took up the matter in the press, the Minister admitted that the Central Government was surprised at the report they had received from the State Government that although forty-one inspections had been carried out and twenty-four people prosecuted, there was not a single case of child labour in the pottery industry (Times of India,12 April 1988).

What seems clear from this brief study is that child labour is a fairly new phenomenon in the pottery industry of Khurja largely because of the need to mass-produce goods at low cost. The traditional Khurja potter did not have a very large market and therefore did not need children. Children only worked as part of apprenticeship training and long with getting regular education.

But with changing technology and the use of moulds, it became possible for such people to enter the pottery industry as had no background of pottery. It was also possible then to hire unskilled labour to do jobs which hitherto required specialized skills- e.g. the technique of moulding clay on the potter's wheel. Once the new technology came in, the demand for the goods grew along with an easy availability of cheap labour and this made Khurja a well-known pottery centre. The changes in the pottery industry also came at a time when in the rural areas mechanization of agriculture, the introduction of electricity and better technology created a class of rural unemployed youth who could not find sustenance in the villages. They flocked to the town for work and the only employment available was in the potteries. The local towns people found that the wages were so low that most of them tried to seek work outside. It was only when they found it impossible to get other work that they continued in the potteries.

Thus amongst the adults, the local people try to find work outside Khurja, preferably in big cities while Bihari and eastern Uttar Pradesh migrants leave their homes in large numbers in search of work and a livelihood and some end up here. It is Because of a combination of factors that wages and conditions or work in the pottery industry are so bad. Low wages has meant in turn that families have to send their children-out to work in order to sustain the family.

Obviously, the children who need help are economically and socially from the lowest strata of society. They are the most vulnerable to exploitation and are in fact working like machines for the profit of others. None of the work they do is of the type that leads to the acquiring of skills which may lead to better prospects and can thus be justifies. If anything, the wages paid to adults who had started working as children are a little less than those who do the same work but entered the work-force at a later stage.

The conditions of most factories in Khurja are not so different from those described by Marx obtaining in the potteries of nineteenth-century England . In fact, Marx has been frequently cited in this study in order to draw attention to what is likely to happen to potters in Khurja in another or one or two generations. The pottery industry of Khurja that employs child labour is relatively new and some of its ill-effects may not be noticed except in a later generation. But the reports from England in the nineteenth-century need to be taken seriously in order to prevent the same kind of consequences!

The pottery industry does not need child labour except as a source of cheap labour. Compulsory education strict child labour laws will go a long way to remove child labour from the pottery industry in India as has been the case in England and Japan. There is nothing a child can do that cannot be done by an adult. But the children who come to work do so because of abject poverty. The only solution is to provide them with free, stipendiary primary education and find alternative employment opportunities for their unemployed or under-employed parents. There are laws against employing children in factories which need to be strictly implemented and employers employing children strictly penalized. The industry will not collapse if children are withdrawn from the work-force. It will only provide more work opportunities for adults.

Bibliography

Achaarya, Poromesh, 'Child Labour' in Seminar, July 1982, 275.

Anand, A.L., 'Export of Locks and Padlocks' in Souventir for Seminar on Locks, Aligarh, 21 March 1982.

Aness, Mohammad, 'Epidemiology of Chest Diseases in Lock Workers in Aligarh (Uttar Pradesh)', Thesis for M.D. Department of Preventive and Social Medicine, Jawaharlal Nehru Medical Collage, (Aligarh: Aligarh Muslim University) 1978.

Anklesaria, Shahnaz, 'Child Delinquents: Rebels without a Cause', Statesman, 8 April 1984.

Arimpoor, Joe, 'Street Children of Madras: A Situational Analysis', Study conducted for Ministry of Welfare, Government of India and UNICEF (Noida: National Labour Institute, Child Labour Cell) 1992.

Arora, Ramesh, The Lock Times (Hindi) (Aligarh: All India Lock Manufacturers Association) August 1986.

Arora, U.P. et al Social Cost of Bonded Labour (Allahabad: Academy of Social Sciences) 1977.

Awachat, Anil, 'The Warp and the Weft-I' in Economic and Political Weekly , vol. XXIII, no. 34, 20 August 1988.

Awasthi, Dilip, 'Glass Industry. Cutting Corners' in India Today, 31 December 1986.

Banerjee, Sumanta, 'Child Labour in India' in Maisteam, vol. XVIII, no. 10, 24 Novermber 1979.

Barse, Sheela, 'Child Labour Hit by Powerloom Closure', Indian Express, 15 November 1985.

——, 'Glass Factories of Firozabad-I. Children Playing with Fire', Indian Express, 5 April 1986a.

——, 'Glass Factories of Firozabad-II. Fleecing of Hapless Labour', Indian Express, 6 April 1986b.

Barse, Sheela, 'Glass Factories of Firozabad-III. Nelson's Eye to Workers' Safety', Indian Express, 8 April 1986c.

Bhat, Ela, 'The Invisibility of Home-based Work. The Case of Piece-rate Workers in India' in Andrea Menefee Singh and Anita Kelles-Vitanen (eds) Invisible Hands (New Delhi: Sage Public cations) 1987.

Bhattacharjee, A., 'The Girl Child: A Being that does not Exist for the Media', Paper presented at the NMC-UNICEF Media Workshop on the Girl Child, New Delhi, 12-14 October 1985.

Bhattacharya, T.P., Status Report on Ceramic Industry at Kburja, U.P. (Calcutta: Central Glass and Ceramics Research Institute) March 1982.

Bhowmik, Sharit K., 'Plantation Labour Act and Child Labour' in Economic and Political Weekly, vol. XXVII, no. 42, 17 October 1992.

Bond, Tim, 'The Abuse of Child Labour in Thailand', An M.R.G. Special Report presented to the Working Group on Slavery; A U.N. Sub-Commission on Human Rights, Geneva, August 1982, pp.1-14.

Bouhdiba, Abdelwahab, 'Exploitation of Child Labour', Special Rapporteur of the Sub-Commission on Prevention of Discrimination and Protection of Minorities, E/CN4/ Sub.2/479, 1981.

Burra, Neera, 'Child Labour in India: Poverty, Exploitation and Vested Interest' in Social Action, vol.36, July-September 1986a.

——, 'Glass Factories of Firozabad: I - Plight of Child Worker-s'in Economic and Political Weekly, vol. XXI, no. 46, 15 November 1986b.

——, 'Glass Factories of Firozabad: II - Plight of Child Workers' in Economic and Political Weekly, vol. XXI,no. 47, 22 November 1986c.

——, A Report on Child Labour in the Lock Industry of Aligarh, Uttar Padesh , India , Prepared for UNICEF (New Delhi) 1987a.

——, A Report on Child Labour in the Gem Polishing Industry of Jaipur, Rajasthan, India , Prepared for UNICEF (New Delhi) 1987b.

——, A Report on Child Labour in the Pottery Industry of Khurja, Uttar Pradesh, India , Prepared for DANIDA (New Delhi) 1987c.

Burra, Neera, 'You've Got your Facts Wrong Mr Tytler', The Times of India, 4 April 1988.

——, The Informalisation of Employment: Child Labour in Urban Industries of India, Labour Market Analysis and Employment Planning, Working Paper no. 25 (Geneva: International Labour Office) 1988.

——, Child Labour in the Brass Ware Industry of Moradabad, India (New Delhi: ILO/ARTEP) 1989.

Census of India, 1981, 'Primary Census Abstracts: General Population', Series 1, Part II 15 (1).

——, 'Provisinol Population Totals: Workers and their Distribution', Series 1, Paper 3, November 1991.

Chadha, T.S. (ed),Carpet Council News (New Delhi: Carpet Export Promotion Council) June 1986.

Chakrapani, S., 'Child Labour in Mandsaur, Slate-Pencil Industry' Recommendations made at Workshop on Child Labour in India (New Delhi: Indian Social Institute) 14-15 November 1985.

Champakalakshmi, R.Measures for Improving the Working Conditions of Children in the Carpet and Glass Bangle Industries Confidential document (New Delhi: Institute of Applied Manpower Research) (n.d.) pp. 1-26.

Chandrasegaran, K., Study on Child Employment in Match Industries and Fireworks at Sivakashi (Pondicherry: Government Law Collage) unpublished (n.d.).

Chanthanom, Suvajee, 'Child Servitude in India' in Child Workers in Asia, vol. 5, no. 5, July-September 1989, pp. 3-8.

Chatteerji, Debasish, 'Child Labour in Glass Industry' in Surya India, June 1986.

Chaudhure, M., 'Sex Bias in Child Nutrition', Paper presented at the NMC-UNICEF Meida Workshop on The Girl Child New Delhi, 12-14 October 1985.

Chowdhury, Neeraj, 'Those Bonded and Branded in Boyhood', Statesman, 11 April 1984a.

——, 'Uttar Pradesh, Bihar Told to Probe into "Bonded" Child Labourers', Patriot, 24 October 1985.

——, 'Bonded Child Weavers Released', Patika, 10 December 1985.

Daniel, Christopher, 'Child Worker has Come to Stay? in Social Welfare, vol. XXII., no. 8, 1976.

Das, M., 'Bonded Child Labour in Mirzapur: 75,000 Kids Exploited in Carpet Industry' in Current, 21 December 1985.

Dasgupta, Saibal, 'Child Labour, Dirt being Swept under the Carpet', Times of India (Bombay) 12 August 1992.

Devi, Mahasveta, 'Palamau: The Long Road to Freedom', Business standard, 21 April 1984a.

——,'MPs Concern over Child Labour', Indian Express, 25 April 1984b.

Gangrade, K.D. and Joseph A. Gathia, Women & Child Workers in the Unorganized Sector (New Delhi: Concept Publishing Company) 1983.

Ganguly, Piyus, 'Child Labour Rules Flouted with Impunity', The Telegraph (Calcutta) 16 April 1984.

Garg, R.B.L., 'Fair Deal for Children', Patriot , 28 November 1980.

Ghosh, A., Street Children of Calcutta: A Situational Analysis, Study conducted for Ministry of Welfare, Government of India and UNICEF (Noida: National Labour Institute, Child Labour Cell) 1992.

Gore, M.S., 'Opening Adress' in Usha Naidu and Kamini R.Kapadia (eds), Child Labour and Health: Problems and Prospects (Bombay: Tata Institute of Social Sciences) 1985.

Government of India, Legislative Assembly Debates (Official

Report) vol. I, Part I, First Session of the Legislative Assembly (Delhi: Superintendent, Government Printing Press) 1921.

——, Report of the Commission on Labour in India (Calcutta: Government of India Central Publication Branch) 1931.

——, Report of the Committee on Child Labour 1979, Ministry of Labour (Nasik: Printed by the Manager, Government of India Press) 1981.

Government of Uttar Pradesh, Report of the UP Labour Department on child Labour in the Glass Industry of Firozabad, (unpublished) 1986a.

——, A Pilot Project on Child Labourers in Carpet-Weaving, (Varanasi: Government of Uttar Pradesh) (mimeo) 1986b.

Gulati, Leela, Profiles in Female Poverty: A Study of Five Poor Working Women in Kerala (Delhi: Hindustan Publishing Corporation) 1981.

——, Child labour in Kerala's Coir Industry — A Study of a Few Selected Villages (Trivandum: Centre for Development Studies) (unpublished) (n.d.).

Gupta , S., 'Child Labour' in ICCW News Bulletin, vol. XXXIII, no. 3, September 1985.

Iyengar.L.V., 'Where Children Labour and Fathers Despair!' Indian Express, 16 February 1986a.

——, 'Child Labour in the Match Units of Southern Tamil Nadu', Paper presented at a Seminar on Child Labour in India (New Delhi: Indian Social Institute) 9 August 1986b.

——, 'Pyre of Childhood: Child Workers in the Factories of Sivakasi' in Manju Gupta and Klaus Voll (eds), Young Hands at Work: Child Labour in India (Delhi: Lucknow: Atma Ram & Sons) 1987.

Jani, Gaurang, 'Child Workers of Diamond Cutting Industry

in Surat —Some Observations', Paper presented at Workshop on Child Labour in India (New Delhi: Indian Social Institute) 9 August 1986.

——, 'No Sparkle in Gem Workers' Lives', The Hindustan Times, 26 July, 1987.

Jhabvala, Renana and Jennifer Sebstadt, 'To Be Self-Employed... and a Woman', Himmat, vol. 17, no. 15, 1980-1.

Juyal, B.N. et al Child Labour: The Twice Exploited (Varanasi: Gandhian Institute of Studies) 1985.

——, Child Labour and Exploitation in the Carpet Industry: A Mirzapur-Bhadohi Case Study (New Delhi: Indian Social Institute) 1987.

Kapoor, Aditi, 'If We Move Slowly We Were Beaten, Carpet Children Recount Days of Captivity', The Times of India , 6 November 1992.

Karlekar, Malavika, Poverty and Women's Work: A Study of Sweeper Women in Delhi (Delhi: Vikas Publishing House) 1982.

Khan, Shamshad, 'Experiences with the Rehabilitation of Working Children: A Practical Approach', Paper presented at a Seminar on Child Labour and the New Legislation (Srinagar: Friedrich Ebert Foundation) 4-8 May 1987.

Khandekar, Mandakini, A Report on the Situation of Children and Youth in Greater Bombay (Bombay: Tata Institute of Social Sciences) 1970.

Khatu, K.K. et al Working Children in India (Baroda: Operations Research Group) 1983.

Kishwar, Madhu and B. Horowitz, 'Family Life: The Unequal Deal' in M. Kishwar and Ruth Vanita (eds), In Search of Answers: Indian Women's Voices from Manushi (London: Zed Books Ltd.) 1984.

Kothari, S., 'Expliting the Young' in Indian Today, 15 January 1983a.

——, 'Child Labour in India; A Case Study of Sivakasi', Paper presented at AWDI-FES Seminar on The State of Unorganised Labour, 24-7 February 1983b.

——, 'There's Blood on those Matchsticks' in Economic and Political Weekly, vol. XVIII, no. 27, 2 July 1983c.

Krishnakumari, N.S., Child Labour in Bangalore City (Delhi: Published by I.S.P.C.K.) 1985.

Kulkarni, M.N., 'Match-making Children in Sivakasi', Economic and Political Weekly, vol. XVIII, no. 43, 22 October 1985.

Kulshreshta, D.K. and S.K. Sharma, 'Child Labour in Moradabad Metalware Industry', The Economic Times, 19 October 1980.

Child Labour in Brass Ware Industry of Moradabad prepared by Labour Commissioner, U.P., (unpublished) 9 January 1988.

Marla, Sarma, 'Bonded Labour in Medak district (A.P.)' in NLI Bulletin, vol. 3, no. 10, October 1977.

——, Bonded Labour in India: National Survey on the Incidence of Bonded Labour, Final Report (New Delhi: Biblia Impex Private Limited) 1981.

Marx, Karl, Capital Volume I, Introduced by Ernest Mandel (The Pelican Marx Library, Penguin Books in association with New Left Review) [1867] 1982.

McDonald, Hamish, 'India. Boys of Bondage. Child Labour though Banned is Rampant' in Far Eastern Review, 9 July 1992.

Mehta, Manharbhai, 'How Children are Exploited in "Socialist" India' in Organizer, January 1983.

Mehta, Prayag, 'Mortgaged Child Labour of Vellore. Women

Beedi Workers Tale of Woe' in Mainstream, vol. XXII, no. 1,3 September 1983.

Menon, Sadanand, 'Sivkasi: The Little Japan of India', The Times of India (Sunday Magazine) New Delhi, 7 October 1979.

Menon, Geeta, 'Health Problems of Working Children: Some Observations' in Usha Naidu and Kamini Kapadia (eds) Child Labour and Health: Problems and Prospects (Bombay: Tata Institute of Social Sciences) 1985.

Menon, Ramesh, 'Child Workers. The Wages of Innocence' in India Today, 15 February 1986.

Mies, Maria, The Lace Makers of Narsapur. Indian Housewives Produce for the World Market (London: Zed Press) 1982.

——, Assisted by Laliltha k. and Krishna Kumari, Indian Women in Subsistence and Agricultural labour, Women, Work and Development 12 (Geneva: International Labour Office) 1986.

Mitra, N., 'Slave Children of Mandsaur' in Sunday, 15-21 June 1986.

Mohandas, M., 'Beedi Workers in Kerala: Conditions of Life and Work' in Economic and Political Weekly, vol. XV, no. 36, 6 September 1980.

Mundle, Sudipto 'The Bonded of Palamau' in Economic and Political Weekly, vol. XI, no. 18,1 May 1976.

Murthy, N.L. et al 'Child Labour in Agriculture: A Case Study in Andhra Pradesh' in Mainstream, vol. XXIII. no. 49, 3 August 1985.

Naidu, Usha and S. Parasuraman, Health Situation of Working Children in Greater Bombay, WHO sponsored Study Report (Bombay: TISS) 1895.

Naik, J.P. Equality, Quality and Quantity: The Elusive Triangle in Indian Education (New Delhi: Allied Publishers Private Limited) 1975a.

——, Policy and Performance in Indian Education 1947 74, Dr K.G. Saiyidian Memorial Trust, Jamianagar, New Delhi (New Delhi: Orient Longman) 1975b.

——, The Educaiton Commmission and After (New Delhi:Allied Publishers Private Limited) 1982.

Nair, R., 'Education: Why do more Girls Drop Out? in Kurukshetra, 1-15 May 1983.

Nangia, Sudesh, Child Workers in Carpet Weaving Industry in Jammu and Kashmir (with a special emphasis on girls) (New Delhi: Project sponsored by UNICEF, Regional Office for South Central Asia) (mimeo) October 1988.

Nayyar, Rohini, 'Female Participation Rates in Rural India' in Economic and Political Weekly, vol. XXII, no. 51, 19 December 1987.

Ninan, S., 'Carpet Boom Rides on Child labour', The Indian Express, 22 December 1983.

——, 'Weaving a Warped Future', The Indian Express (Sunday Magazine) 6 May 1984a.

——, 'Government is Firm on Ending Child Labour: Minister', The Hindustan Times, 3 May 1984b.

——, 'SC Notices in Mirzapur Case', The Indian Express, 9 May 1984c.

——, 'Dream that Turned into a Harrowing Nightmare', Patriot 11 April 1984d.

——, 'Kids Kidnapped to Weave Carpets', The Indian Express, 11 April 1984e.

Pal, Bulbul, 'Bangle-makers: A Fragile Existence', Express Magazine, 4 May 1986.

Pandit, M.L., Child Labour in Handicrafts of Kashmir Valley (unpublished manuscript) (n.d.).

Pardesi, Ghanshyam, 'Dust unto Dust' in The Illustrated Weekly of India, 11 August 1985.

Parke, J.E., Text-book of Preventive and Social Medicine (Jabalpur: Banarsidas Bhanot) 1974.

Parmeggiani, Luigi, Encyclopaedia of Occupational Health and Safety, Third (Revised edition) vol. 2 (Geneva: International Labour Organization) 1983.

Patel, B.B., Status Report on the Problems of Child Labour with a Focus on Diamond Cutting and Polishing Industry of Gujarat (Carried out at the instance of Ministry of Labour, Government of India) (Ahmedabad: Gandhi Labour Institute) September 1987 (mimeo).

Patel, B.B. and Raksha Alagh, Child Labour in India (Incidence and Occupational Diversification across Social Strata) (Ahmedabad: Gandhi Labour Institute) (n.d.).

Patil, B.R., The Working Children in Bangalore City (Bangalore: Indian Institute of Management) (unpublished manuscript) (n.d.).

——, 'Child Workers in Bangalore-I', The Financial Express (Bombay) 3 January 1986.

Patnaik, Malabika, 'Child Labour in India: Size and Occupational Distribution' in Journal of the Indian Institute of Public Administration, vol. 25, July-December 1979.

Pichholiya, K.R., 'Child Labour in a Metropolitan City: A Study if Ahmedabad' in Indian Journal of Labour Economics, vol. XXII, no. 4, January 1980.

Pillai, Ajith, 'Children of Shuklaji Street', The Sunday observer, 1 September 1985.

Pitt, David C., 'Child Labour and Health' in Usha Naidu and Kamini Kapadia (eds), Child Labour and Health: Problems and Prospects (Bombay: Tata Institute of Social Sciences) 1985a.

——, 'Child Labour and Health' in P.M.Shah and Nigel Cantwell (eds), Child Labour: Threat to Health and Development (2nd revised edition) (Geneva, Switzerland: Published by Defence for Childern International) 1985b.

Prasad,T., 'Preventing Exploitation of Children' in Social Welfare, August 1982.

Prembhai, Report to the Supreme Court regarding Child Weavers of Mirzapur-Bhadohi-Varanasi (Varanasi: mimeo) 1984.

Puri, Rakhat, 'Indian has 100 Million Bonded Labours', The Hindustan Times, 30 September 1984.

Purushotham, P., 'A Profile of Beedi Workers' in Social Change, vol. 13,no. 1, March 1983.

Ramaswamy, S.S. et al Status Report on Child Labour (Ahmedabad: National Institute of Occupational Health) (mimeo) 1987.

Rao, Amiya, 'silicosis Deaths of Slate Workers' in Economic and Political Weekly, vol. XV, no. 44, 1 Novermber 1980.

Rao,B.V.R. and B.Malik, Street Children of Hyderabad: A Situational Analysis (A sutdy conducted for Ministry of Social Welfare, Government of India and UNICEF) (Noida: National Labour Institute, Child Labour Cell) 1992.

Rao, Sudha V., 'Rural Labour: Case Study of a Karnatake village' in Economic and Political Weekly, vol. XIX, no. 18, 5 May 1984.

Rai, Usha, 'The Forgotten Children of Delhi', The Times of India, 16 August 1984.

Ratnani, Jagdish, 'Tender Age, Big Shoulders' in Onlooker, 23 July-7 August 1985.

Reddy, Nandana, Street Children of Bangalore: A Situational Analysis (A study conducted for Ministry of Social Welfare, Government of India and UNICEF) (Noida: National

Labour Institute, Child Labour Cell) 1992.

Sadhu and Singh, 'Child Labour in India' in The Indian Workers, 6 October 1980.

Sarma, A.M., 'Child Labour in Indian Industries' in The Indian Journal of Social Work, vol. XI, no. 3, Ocotober 1979.

Sebastian, A., 'Child Migrants and Child Migrant Labour', in K. Srinivasan et al (eds) Demographic and Socio-economic Aspects of the Child in India (Bombay: Himalaya Publishing House) 1979.

Sengupta, Arindam, 'The Curse of Katni-Limestone Industry Workers Dying through Barbaric Exploitation' in Probe India, June 1983.

Abbreviations

JRY	Jawahar Rojgar Yojna
ICDS	Integrated Child Development Scheme
SNP)	Supplementary Nutrition Programme
MCH	Maternity and Child Health Centres
IRDP	Integrated Rural Development Programme
NREP	National Rural Employment Programme
RLEGP	Rural Landless Employment Guarantee Programme
DWACRA	Development of Women and Children in Rural Areas
SEPUP	Self-Employment Programme for the Urban Poor
DIC)	District Industries Centre
NIDC	National Industrial Development Corporation
ITDC	India Tourism Development Corporation
GT	General Traders
CRRID	Centre for Research in Rural and Industrial Development
ESIC	Employees State Insurance Corporation
MIDS	Madras Institute of Development Studies
AMU	Aligarh Muslim University

Index

E

F

G

H

I